FINDING MARS

Finding Mars

NED ROZELL

UNIVERSITY OF ALASKA PRESS
Fairbanks

University of Alaska Press

P.O. Box 756240

Fairbanks, AK 99775-6240

ISBN 978-1-60223-122-1 (paper); 978-1-60223-123-8 (e-book)

Library of Congress Cataloging-in-Publication Data

Rozell, Ned, 1963–
    Finding Mars / by Ned Rozell.
        p. cm.
    Includes index.
    ISBN 978-1-60223-122-1 (pbk. : alk. paper)
    1. Yoshikawa, K. (Kenji) 2. Scientists—Japan—Biography. 3. Permafrost—
Research—Alaska. 4. Alaska—Climate. I. Title.
    Q143.Y56R69 2011
    551.3'84—dc22   2010028028

Cover design by Dennis Roberts
Cover images by Kenji Yoshikawa: (front) Kenji's tent in the Sahara under a starry sky;
        (back) Canada's High Arctic from the air.
Interior design and layout by Rachel Fudge
Maps by Rick Britton Cartography

This publication was printed on acid-free paper that meets the minimum require-
ments for ANSI / NISO Z39.48–1992 (R2002) (Permanence of Paper for Printed
Library Materials).

SNOWY OWL BOOKS
an imprint of the University of Alaska Press

Contents

Acknowledgments

This book has taken me places I never imagined, from a whale-watching perch made of sea ice north of Barrow to a steamy Okinawa bar patrolled by a dachshund. Thanks to Kenji Yoshikawa for leading me to these places, and many more, and for inspiring me with his constant example of dreaming big.

Special thanks to Dan White, head of the University of Alaska's Institute of Northern Engineering, who walked in one day and suggested this fun project at the perfect time. He, more than anyone else, made this book happen, with financial support and innovative thinking that is often not the norm in a university setting. He found a detour around every roadblock, often with that delightful phrase "No worries."

Masayuki Matsubara, Kenji's friend and partner across Antarctica, said one night in Tokyo that he would send me a copy of an unpublished manuscript he had written on Kenji's life. A few months later, a disc arrived in my mailbox. Matsubara-san wrote an excellent book, and I'm thankful he shared it with me. It revealed to me a Kenji I could not have known otherwise, and added depth to this book.

I thank Larry Hinzman, director of the International Arctic Research Center, for first telling me about Kenji way back when. Larry urged me to meet Kenji, and Larry supported this book both with funding and with the space to write it. He covered the excellent translation work of Yuri Bult-Ito, for which I am also grateful.

Thanks for early guidance go to Elisabeth Dabney of the University of Alaska Press, who with sharp instinct saved me from myself many times. Brian Keenan combed the manuscript on deadline and skillfully removed a few tangles.

Thanks to Kathy Berry Bertram for being my longtime friend and boss and for suggesting the trip that pulls along the narrative of this book. Thanks to my immediate supervisor, Amy Hartley of the Geophysical Institute, for her steadfast encouragement and understanding as a fellow writer.

Akio Hachinohe was generous with his time and his funds after Kenji and I visited his old friend in Hokkaido. Big thanks to Kenji's parents, Tadao and Yuko Yoshikawa, and all his friends throughout Japan who hosted us on our visit. I am grateful they all made time for interviews.

BP supported this book with a generous grant via the University of Alaska. Daniel Julius, vice president of academic affairs, was key in making that happen. UAF also provided other types of support, and I hope this book shines a good light on an institution that has been part of my life for more than twenty years.

A note about photos: Uncredited shots in the book are mine, except for one of Fridtjof Nansen, another of Nansen and Hjalmar Johansen, and a third of Nansen's ship, the *Fram*.

Finally, an apology to those I've missed here, for my memory on deadline isn't always the sharpest. But here's one last remembrance: a big thank you to my wife and daughter, Kristen and Anna, who were huddling by an electric heater in a nine-by-nine-foot cabin with two dogs when I was buzzing through western Alaska with Kenji. Thank you for unusual patience and enduring love.

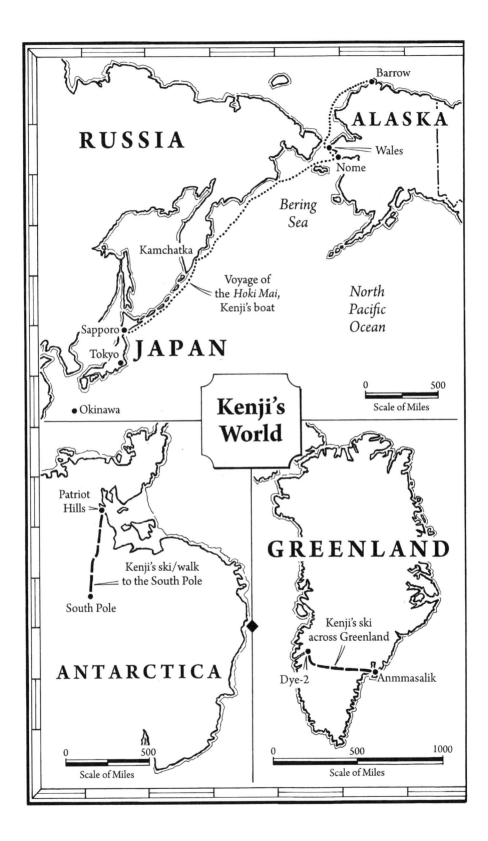

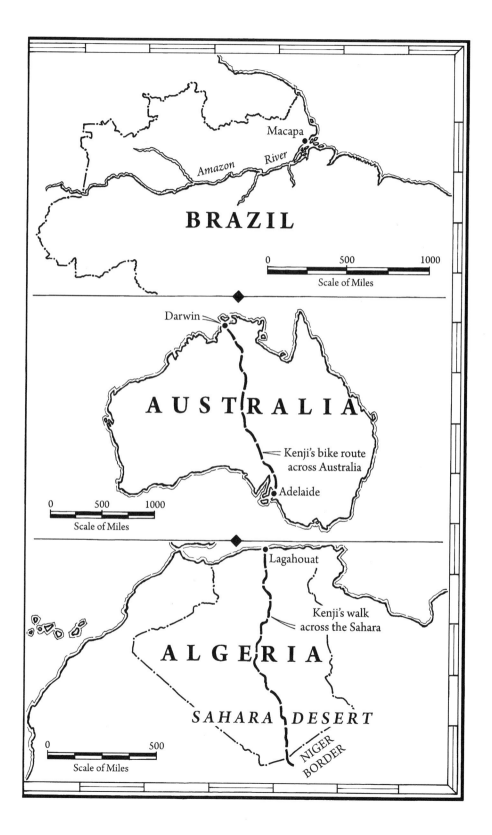

BRAZIL

Macapa

Amazon River

0   500   1000
Scale of Miles

AUSTRALIA

Darwin

Kenji's bike route
across Australia

Adelaide

0   500   1000
Scale of Miles

ALGERIA

Lagahouat

Kenji's walk
across the Sahara

SAHARA DESERT

NIGER
BORDER

0   500
Scale of Miles

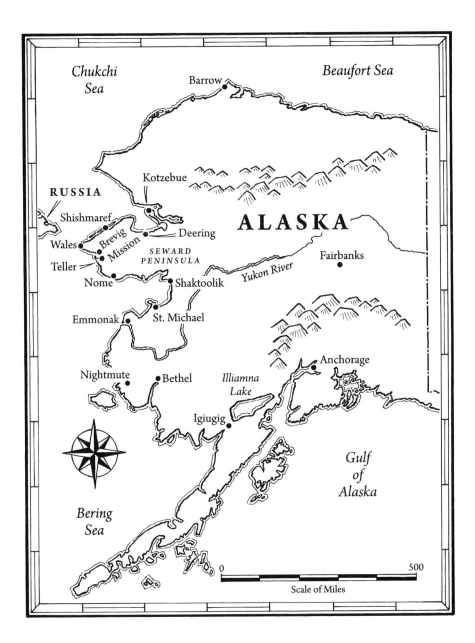

*I*f you start from upstream to down, you are sure of where you go. You always go to the ocean, no choice.

If you start from mouth of Amazon, you have thousands of chances to go somewhere else. Life is this way, right? Upstream. You don't know which way you go. Sometimes you have a right to choose.

Sometimes it's not you. God, or somebody else, choose. I want to test my destiny. The unknown is much funner than downstream.

—Kenji Yoshikawa

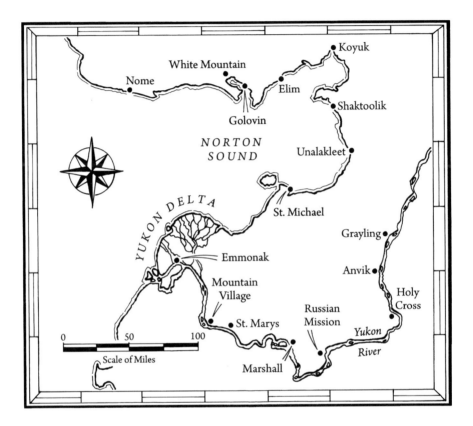

Chapter One

Not Like the Other Boys

Beneath us, the broad mouth of the Yukon River is snowy and gray and fuzzy and soft, like a lens I can't twist into focus. In front of us, two thousand feet in the air, visibility is not good, and the cab of this Cessna smells like gas and hot electronics. These conditions make me glad I am not the pilot, and aware that I am trusting my life to a complete stranger wearing a baseball cap and leather jacket. It's a risk we all accept because there's no other way to go from the Kuskokwim River to the Yukon in just a few hours.

Tohru points to a dark L etched into the black-and-white world below us. Over the drone of the Cessna, he turns and mouths the words "St. Marys," which conjures images of the upstate New York church where my older brother eulogized my father not long ago, but couldn't be farther away. Tohru recognizes the airstrip and the perpendicular crosswind strip because he and Kenji snowmobiled to the Yup'ik village from Manley Hot Springs during the past year. St. Marys was the final stop on a bitter eight-hundred-mile spring trip, during which they passed Iditarod mushers who were ducking behind their sleds to cut a biting headwind. That journey was the most successful of Kenji's science-driven missions into Alaska by snowmobile. This year, he is trying to extend his reach into the Bush. Alaska is a blank map hanging before him, and Kenji is sticking thumbtacks into it with impressive speed.

Kenji, who chartered this flight from Bethel, the hub of southwest Alaska, looks out the window at serpentine rivers, distinguished from the white world of tundra by the dark spruce that cling to the shore like desert palms around

waterholes, which is essentially what they are, except for the latitude and the size of the leaves.

Squinting out the Cessna window, Kenji is probably looking for permafrost features, like the raised domes of pingos, or dimples on the snow surface from thawed ice wedges. These features are obvious to him, but not to Tohru and me. Kenji is always looking for a place to take the Earth's temperature.

It's a hard, cold, lonely world where Alaska's largest river meets the ocean, but when its surface is wet in the summer, the country beneath this airplane attracts millions of beating hearts, large and small. Sinuous liquid channels inhale millions of salmon, bulging with fat that is their only nourishment for a thousand-mile journey upstream. Nesting swans, ducks, sandpipers, and other water-loving birds incubate eggs, at rest after trips from Asia and ponds in the Lower 48. Mosquitoes that outnumber Alaskans by several orders of magnitude whine their way toward anything leaking carbon dioxide.

At this moment, you would be safe from proboscises on the tundra. In mid-March, the landscape is numb. If it weren't for the buzz of this single-engine plane, the surface below, cratered with moose tracks, would be as quiet as the moon.

In the winter season, which occupies most of the year, the Yukon River delta lacks most of the elements humans need to survive, especially warmth. It's an extreme environment most people try to avoid, because it is not comfortable, especially for tropical creatures. The few people born here have it figured out, getting out in this hungry season for ptarmigan and hares, pulling home wood, and getting ready for spring. But most Americans would take a look at the whiteness and the flatness and the lack of trees and agree with William Seward's critics more than a century ago. Just a few souls are attracted to this place; they are descendants in spirit of the restless people who scrambled across the land bridge.

These edges of the world also call out to this mid-forties guy with the blackened thumbnail, shaved head, and concrete-block chest and uncommon power that might leave him the last man standing after a misunderstanding in a dark pub.

In wandering foreign landscapes, Kenji has endured more discomfort than most others he walks past in the Fairbanks grocery store. His successes and failures have endowed him with confidence. Compared to the frozen tundra passing beneath this Cessna, the Sahara was even more lifeless. The South Pole was colder and much windier. In Greenland, his bed was a shelf of ice hundreds of feet thick, and, in a frozen saltwater lagoon north of Alaska, the distorted moon rising like an orange potato was the brightest light he'd seen for months, as he overwintered on a stranded boat. There, he was totally delighted to be alone. For a man whose childhood aspiration was to go to Mars, Kenji has slept many nights on its sister landscapes.

His search for Mars on Earth is an ongoing quest; Kenji has never been to the community he will visit today. Emmonak—"Emo" to the locals—is a village of about 850 people on a sluggish artery of the Yukon known as Kwiguk Pass. Home mostly to Yup'ik people and a few non-Natives, Emmonak is about twelve miles from the spot where the Yukon empties into the Bering Sea. Except for the bank of the river, which is steep enough for village kids to use as a sledding hill, Emmonak is as flat as prairie. On U.S. Geological Survey maps lakes near the village have the number 5 in them, for feet above sea level. A little bit southwest, Nunavakanuk Lake's surface shows "−4," an oddity in Alaska reminiscent of Death Valley (which Kenji recently visited, drilling a hole at Badwater to record the temperatures experienced by that baked ground, which once reached 201 degrees Fahrenheit).

In Emmonak, Kenji, Tohru Saito, and I will start a nine-hundred-mile trip by snowmobile from the mouth of the Yukon to the mouth of the Noatak. After covering four degrees of latitude, we'll stop at the Arctic Circle, and the town of Kotzebue.

Our lead traveler, Kenji Yoshikawa, is a scientist with the University of Alaska in Fairbanks. He studies permafrost soil, ice, woolly mammoth, buried people, or anything else that remains frozen for two years or more. Not coincidentally, a robot arm recently pried permafrost soil from the surface of Mars. Both Mars and Earth are far enough from the sun that some of their valleys and mountains stay colder all year than about water's freezing temperature. Repeat those conditions for a few hundred years, and you've grown an impressive bed of permafrost. Alaska's North Slope has that solid foundation, with soil frozen for thousands of feet below the twelve inches of surface tundra that softens each year in summer. Kenji has chosen this mysterious subject as his life's scientific exploration.

On travels around the world, Kenji, who was born in 1963, has always included an element of science to make his trips more meaningful. He learned on a trip to New Zealand that he does not make a good tourist; a mission makes him happy: the more problems that stretch his mind and body, the better.

On this journey, he wants to see what parts of western Alaska remain frozen during the summer. Other scientists have speculated as to where the permafrost is out here, and some have made scattered measurements, but nobody knows the whole story. Like many scientific disciplines in Alaska, the study of permafrost is in its infancy. Scientists like the resourceful Ernest Leffingwell—who lived in a sod hut on Alaska's North Slope long after his government funding ran out—recognized permafrost in the early decades of the 1900s, and noted that Eskimos dug cellars into the substance to preserve food. It wasn't until decades later, during World War II, that military scientists were eager to see what sort of tactical advantage could be gained by utilizing ground that is rock-hard all year. Due to infiltration of manmade warmth and radiation from the sun, putting heated buildings and roads right on top of permafrost soil was not cost-effective, they found. The maintenance costs of a structure soar when its foundation sinks a foot on one side, inches on the other, or when your road, in its second summer of existence, runs through a thaw pond. But permafrost could also be useful for creating tunnels in hillsides, portals that would retain their structure with minimal buttressing, so long as there was an insulated plug at the door.

No one has much of an idea of what the permafrost map might look like in western Alaska. Kenji wants to draw it. He has designed a trek where he will tow his drilling equipment from village to village on a tack up Alaska's wind-scoured west coast, home to not many people and fewer trees. Using a drill powered by a small generator and forced into frozen soil by his shoulders and back, Kenji will dig boreholes as deep as twenty feet at each village. He will then drop in plastic pipe to prevent the two-inch-diameter holes from collapsing on the tiny thermometers attached to a cable. The thermometers, designed to record temperatures for years, will tell Kenji whether an area has permafrost and, of great importance to him, how warm or cold it is. "Warm" permafrost, that within a degree of thawing, is widespread in Alaska. People like me, who drive and live over it, will miss it if it goes.

Kenji's goal is to create a baseline temperature measurement of a very-stable-but-changeable substance that scientists can reference fifty years from now. He hopes some of the Native children who see him working might become those scientists, or at least have a memory of the time when a Japanese Alaskan came to the village by snowmobile in winter and drilled a hole in the ground.

Kenji's schedule is, as always, ambitious: Emmonak, Kotlik, Stebbins, St. Michael, Unalakleet, Shaktoolik, Koyuk, Elim, Golovin, White Mountain, Nome, Teller, Brevig Mission, Wales, Shishmaref, Deering, Kotzebue. Seventeen villages in all, on the Yukon Delta, the Bering Sea coast, and the Chukchi Sea, with only sixteen days for the trip. Most scientists would budget in a few extra days for weather. Kenji is weatherproof.

. . .

One thousand Iditarod dogs have already passed on part of the route, giving us a good chance of a nice marked trail from Unalakleet to Nome. There are few trails as pleasing in texture—firm, but softened by leathery paws—as the path packed down by dozens of dog teams. Their frozen excretions sometimes pose a hazard for skiers because of a reduced coefficient of friction, but these spots do not slow snowmobiles. The trip will also include hundreds of miles of trails that are not the Iditarod. These winter trails, historic routes traveled in the frozen months, sometimes show up on USGS maps as dashed lines. In reality, these paths snake around from year to year, according to the location of the smoothest snow and ice and the whims of the trailbreaker. Some years, the trails aren't there at all.

Kenji has set up a scenario in which three snowmobiles ("snowmachines" in Alaska, and hereafter on these pages) will be waiting for us in Emmonak, along with two unbreakable plastic sleds to carry all the gear and drilling equipment to set up permafrost observatories in each of the villages. Our plan, when we land in Emmonak, is to find a spot that holds promise for permafrost (pipe cleaner black spruce are often a giveaway of poorly drained, frozen ground beneath), drill a hole through the moss and into the soil beneath these trees, and insert sensors attached to little data loggers. Then we can arrange in heavy-duty ActionPacker storage bins all the gear that has arrived from Fairbanks via Anchorage, gas up the snowmachines with $5.91-per-gallon village fuel, sleep at the school on a classroom floor, and, in the morning, take off on a permafrost crusade.

Other scientists aspiring to get the same data might have opted for a chartered plane that could leapfrog from village to village. That is a sensible, efficient approach. But Kenji knows the weak point of small aircraft out here—blowing snow often makes flying dangerous or impossible. Hugging the ground is more dependable in this country of big winds, and "snogos," as some locals call them, also lend more credibility to Kenji's task than if he were to drop in from the sky. And driving yourself from village to village is a lot more fun.

After about an hour in the air and 120 miles from Bethel, the pilot somehow knows it is time to bank hard left, over another frozen channel of the Yukon. Slowly, a group of buildings comes into focus through the haze. Emmonak is a village of about two hundred houses, on three or four streets that bend with the river. From the air, we see the larger buildings in the village—the school and the community center—and huge warehouses lining the Yukon upriver, for processing the straight-from-the-ocean-and-dripping-with-Omega-3 kings and chums during the commercial salmon harvest.

On the term *village*: its connotation in Alaska is unlike that in the rest of the United States, where one might picture a tidy burg of soccer moms and Little League fields and mostly white people living in nice homes with decent cars out front. Alaska has more than two hundred villages, most of them on rivers, very few on the road system. Most of Alaska's seven hundred thousand people have never been to a village, and will never go. The main residents of Alaska's villages are Indian (the Athabaskans of Interior Alaska and Tlingits and Haida of Southeast) and Yupik and Inupiaq (of the western and northern coasts). An average-size village has a few hundred people, most of them "Natives," the term for Eskimos or Indians. A village probably has one or two stores, windowless buildings that stock the basics, along with junk food, soda, sometimes four-wheelers (known as "Hondas"), and outboard motors. Many Alaska villages are dry or "damp," with the importation of alcohol prohibited. Most villages have a community center that is often round and traditional in design, a church or two, and a huge, modern school, which is often the resting place for travelers, because few villages have hotels. Many have no restaurants, either, so visitors get to know the village stores.

Villages are often in settings that can be described as stunning (Wales, where the continental divide meets the ocean at the spine of a hogback of black rock), but they often feature living conditions that would make most people from Anchorage cringe. Homes are practical and more often than not unfinished or in need of renovation; blood from harvested animals on the plywood floor is accepted, and perhaps even a source of pride. If you are a dog lover, it helps to switch off your sensitivities when visiting villages, because it's a tough life out there of short chains and no escape from the shit or the kicks from children or the wind. The people out there are often beautiful and sad and hopeful and caught in a clash of cultures that was not their choice. My common thought in villages is that this person has a lot to teach me, but I feel unworthy to ask. I also feel a twinge of guilt for my white comfortable upbringing when I visit the villages, and I don't know how to resolve this. But villagers often disarm you with gentle talk, soft nods, and a bowl of moosehead soup.

Though small willows and shrubs cling to Emmonak like stubble, treeless tundra extends northward as far as the curvature of the Earth allows you to see. From a hundred feet above, the village looks like an island of straight chainsaw cuts amid an ocean of white, the latter best suited for voles and foxes.

But the March view is an illusion of scarcity here in the Yukon River delta. In summer, people scatter from the villages into fish camps along the river, all the way from its mouth to Mountain Village, seventy miles upriver, about two hours by boat. Along this waterway, they net salmon as long as their arms. Then they split them to the tail and hang them over smoky alder fires to preserve them, keep the flies off, and enhance their flavor. When the sun is high in the sky, a good portion of this deceptive landscape has people walking and boating on it, and the delta delivers pounds of protein and gobs of fat.

■ ■ ■

As we glide above the runway, the pilot lowers his flaps. We grimace for the impact of chilled rubber wheels on gravel. Clutch. Wait for the bounce. Exhale.

A glimpse out the window shows three snowmachines sitting outside a steel-sided building. A shipping company flew them from Fairbanks to Anchorage to Emmonak for Kenji. But something is missing.

Our glimpse of the equipment hints at an early challenge of the trip—two of the three snowmachines were to have large plastic sleds attached to them, in order to accommodate the drilling gear we will be towing across western Alaska. We see no sleds.

The instant the plane's propeller spins to a halt, Kenji is out the door and into the cold air. After we unload our stuff from the wing compartments, Kenji sprints, head down like a bull, to where the snowmachines are sitting. Tohru and I follow at a slower pace in our weighty snowmachining clothes, designed to make you impervious to a thirty-mile-per-hour wind at thirty below.

"No good," he says when we catch up. "No sleds."

Another building nearby looks deserted, but a Native man wearing a parka and a baseball cap with the logo of a satellite Internet company answers Kenji's rap on the door. We walk inside the warehouse and see most of the gear—but, alas, not a sled in sight.

Kenji heads back outside, jumps on a snowmachine, and, after a few pulls, starts it. In a detonation of blue smoke, he thumbs the throttle and heads toward a village he hasn't visited before. He is wearing no hat, and the bright spring sunshine reflects off his olive head as he disappears around a building on a zero-degree day.

"Where's he going?" I ask Tohru.

Tohru, who has lived this scene more than once, shakes his head.

"I don't know. Probably to look for a place to drill."

. . .

Like birds that migrate through the blackness of night using stars, Earth's magnetic field, their eyes, and God knows what else, some people are born with an internal compass. A slant of sunlight warming his shoulder is useful information; the wind kissing his cheek leads to a subtle route adjustment; mountains on a map quickly match up to mountains visible through the haze; stars evoke a feeling of security. And, as the first molecules of salt settle into receptors within his nostrils, Kenji thinks ocean.

Kenji Yoshikawa was born into a warm, damp landscape where he was rarely alone. The western Tokyo section called Higashimurayama in which he grew up is home to three thousand people per square mile; Alaska has slightly more than one person for every square mile. He lived with his parents and older brother in a two-story house a few feet from other houses, each with laundry draped over railings, drying slowly in the moist wind. The Yoshikawas' neighborhood sprung up when Japan prepared to show off its recovery from World War II as the world descended upon Tokyo for the 1964 Olympics.

Today, Honda and Nissan vans squeeze into their covered parking spaces with inches to spare on each side. There seems not a square foot of wasted space, nor room for sloppiness. Even the small fruit trees and sculpted shrubs are orderly.

Two-story houses cluster amid a honeycomb of narrow streets, upon which roll small new cars (a Prius is a large car here) and many people on bicycles. Sidewalks are spotless, with concrete power poles sprouting from them, and many houses border narrow plots of land tended for vegetables. The landscape is utilitarian, with no trace of wildness other than rows of ginkgo and other trees along roadways and clumped in small parks. Birds adapted to an urban environment sing from branches and rooftops.

Greater Tokyo is home to about thirty-five million souls, many of whom commute by train to the center of the city, swelling its population by day and shrinking it by nightfall as they leave. (Contrast that thirty-five million with the one hundred thousand people who live in the same approximate space in the Fairbanks North Star Borough, where Kenji now lives.)

The Tokyo trains are where a person realizes that he or she is in the most populated urban center on the planet, especially during the early-morning and after-work rush hours. Then, seconds after the doors open, the trains fill to capacity with warm, well-dressed humanity. The final riders politely shove backward into others as the automatic doors clip their pant legs. This amoeba of life moves along, each person pushed up against several others, each in total silence except for the ticking of phone keys, as people compose text messages (speaking on cell phones is prohibited on the trains; everyone complies). Train stations are strikingly clean, with uniformed attendants wiping down escalator rails and walls, and sometimes mopping the subway floors.

Photo courtesy Kenji Yoshikawa

Like a cleaner version of New York's Times Square, central Tokyo is a techie's paradise, where a person can find all the latest computers, pitched by smiling salespeople in chaotic, colorful storefronts. The city core is a model of function: all the vending machines, magnetic train ticket readers, and parking meters work, and the busiest trains open their doors for boarding every few minutes, at their promised time of arrival.

Due to government rules that require more frequent (and expensive) inspections for older cars, the streets are flooded with new, small models. People have no space to park big cars, and no U.S.-made models are on the streets. But a visual sweep of central Tokyo reveals several of America's most successful businesses that cater to busy people: Kentucky Fried Chicken, McDonald's, and Subway.

Into the world's most populated metropolitan area came Kenji Yoshikawa, on May 16, 1963. His mother, Yuko, worked as a secretary for a company that makes fiberglass pipes. With prominent cheekbones and a youthful face that hasn't aged much when compared to photos of forty years ago, Yuko enjoys creating works of ceramic and doting on her two papillon dogs, energetic bouncers of shin height with intelligent faces and long fur that absorbs petting hands. The dogs, whose flared ears make them resemble butterflies (*papillon* in French), explode with sharp barks at the ring of the doorbell. Yuko displays more photos of the dogs in her home's common areas than of her two sons, including a shot of two dogs sharing a chair in front of a birthday cake.

Kenji's father, Tadao, worked for Bridgestone Tires for a few decades before retiring with his health and vitality intact. In addition to showering affection

upon the two dogs (so much that he has built carpeted runways leading to the dashboard in his Nissan van), he enjoys making precise wood cuts with a scroll saw, fashioning, among other things, cutouts of small elephants, giraffes, pigs, and dogs. At the entrance to the home is a wooden dachshund with "Yoshikawa" and address numbers on its midsection, along with several ceramic plaques emblazoned by Yuko with the family name and "Welcome" in English.

Born in 1937, as was his wife, Tadao has an easy smile and traces of gray in his black hair. Neither Yuko nor Tadao are as tall as their youngest son, and there is no hint of where Kenji inherited his barrel chest and wrestler's build, nor his insatiable hunger to see the world.

For a reason unknown to his parents, young Kenji showed an early desire to travel. His favorite schoolbook was a world atlas, which he still owns. As a child, he stared at maps of the Sea of Japan and the East China Sea and wondered if they were somehow different, these seemingly connected oceans with different names. He loved to look up at the blue sky near the horizon where it lightened a bit and dream of what extraordinary landscape was beneath it. Maybe the deserts of Australia, the ones he had seen in his atlas? Images of sand dunes and icebergs kept him awake as he lay in bed at night.

The first manifestation of Kenji's wanderlust occurred when he was in third grade. For months, he had a destination in mind—his grandmother's house, about six miles away. He also had the means—a bicycle with a leaky rear tire.

When his parents left for work one day, Kenji put his plan into action, rolling his bicycle out of the house. Remembering the soft tire, he grabbed a hand pump.

He pinched the pump between his left hand and the handlebar, and he rolled away on the gravel road. He felt like he was flying, as untethered as the tree sparrows flitting above.

After a few minutes of exquisite freedom, he pulled over and glanced up and down the street, expecting some adult to jump out and end his fun. But no one stopped him.

He kept heading west, keeping the sun on his left temple, following the roads his father had driven when they visited his grandmother. He recognized stores and railroad crossings he had seen while riding in the backseat of the family car. He rolled ahead, his stomach tingling with fear and excitement.

He pedaled through the busy streets, still amazed that no one made an effort to stop a four-foot boy as he moved alone down the road. He looked down at his mushy tire, pulled over to the sidewalk, and pumped some life into it. Then, he straddled his bike and continued on.

After an hour, Kenji arrived at his grandmother's house, flushed with pride but also apprehensive that his grandmother might scold him for his boldness.

Feeling sheepish, he leaned his bike against his grandmother's house. He knocked on her door, his heart beating faster than it had on his ride. He heard no movement inside. He knocked again. Nothing. His grandmother wasn't home.

After such a daring feat, the most likely next step for a nine-year-old would be to call his parents, or at least pump up his bike tire and turn for home.

Instead, Kenji pointed his bike toward the sun and another remembered route. About once a year, his family would visit his aunt and uncle's place near Hino City, another densely populated section of Tokyo, twenty miles from his grandmother's house.

Kenji pedaled and pumped, dismounting his bike to cross major highways as he felt his way along. Recognizing things he had seen before—temples, parks, the bridge over the Tama River—made him feel relieved, excited, and a little proud. They were new feelings, and he liked them.

After hours of riding and inflating his tire at regular intervals, he turned up a familiar street to the house of his cousin, Yuki Harada.

Yuki was playing with a friend in a house next door to her own. Through the open window, she heard a familiar but out-of-place voice calling out to her. *Kenji?*

She looked outside and saw him, steadying his bike with his pump still in hand. She looked around for his parents' car, but didn't see it.

"Ken-chan!" she yelled. "Are you by yourself?"

"Yes," Kenji said.

When Yuki's parents returned home, they were puzzled to see the strange bike outside and, inside, their nephew. Kenji's uncle asked him how he had known the complicated thirty-mile route to their home, which he had only visited a few times before.

"I learned how to get here by riding in my father's car," Kenji said. "I didn't know the street names—I just had a feeling."

His uncle tried not to smile as he picked up the phone and dialed Kenji's father, whose eyes widened at the news that his son was halfway across Tokyo.

Tadao, seeing it was rush hour, decided against driving. He caught a train bound for Hino City, wondering what he should say to his son after such a risky venture. Was this an occasion for discipline? Or guarded praise?

As the magnitude of his adventure set in after describing his ride to his aunt and uncle, Kenji saw his father walking up the street. He braced for the worst, not knowing how his father would react to this act of independence.

As his father walked up the sidewalk, Kenji felt both relief and a fearful anticipation of his father's reaction.

Moved by his son's pondering eyes, Tadao hugged him.

"You had a fun time today, didn't you?" he said.

Kenji's face lit up.

"Yes, and I never once got lost!"

Kenji hugged his cousin, and then his aunt and uncle, who now had a story to tell their friends at tea time. They couldn't imagine their daughter making a solo trip of one mile, much less thirty.

Tadao thanked his brother-in-law and led Kenji out the door. They left the bike as a gift for Kenji's cousin.

"Now that you've ridden this far, you must be hungry," Tadao said.

At a restaurant, a rare indulgence for the Yoshikawas, Tadao got the details of the ride. He smiled, listened, and wondered where his son got the gumption for such an expedition. Hearing Kenji's enthusiastic chatter, Tadao confirmed a belief he'd had since Kenji was a baby—that his son was different from most Japanese people. He also had a feeling that the bike adventure was just the beginning.

Returning home, Kenji burst inside and into a long hug from Yuko.

As she squeezed her chubby little son, she too realized that the little adventurer who was so eager to know the world would continue to explore it, regardless of how much she and Tadao wanted to protect him. She called the ride their first "surprise" from Kenji.

■ ■ ■

His appetite whetted by the success of his ride, Kenji soon expanded his web throughout Tokyo. He had a new bike, with racing-style curled handlebars, five gears, and directionals that blinked with the help of a battery pack.

His parents both worked Saturdays, leaving Kenji and his brother to play with friends. Kenji would make silent plans, wait for his parents to leave, and grab his bike. Knowing he had four hours until they returned, Kenji would ride away from home, always in a new direction, for two hours. At that point, he would turn around and retrace his route. When his parents returned, Kenji would be playing at home.

As the weeks went on, his routes from home became spokes from a hub, and he filled in the map of the world around him. He was so stealthy that his parents never knew of his Saturday explorations.

But Tadao and Yuko were the type of parents who might not have stopped him, even if they could have. They made efforts to nurture his adventurous spirit. When Kenji showed interest in his father's hobby of photography, Tadao drove Kenji outside the city at night to take photos of stars where there was less light pollution. Kenji developed the photos, sometimes taken through a telescope, with his father. He learned the constellations visible from Tokyo, and was surprised and pleased to learn that explorers used stars to navigate. As he got older, Kenji chose to go to a high school that had a dome for observing stars, rather than one closer to home.

Another formative experience for Kenji was his enrollment in the Boy Scouts. He liked to do anything outside, and in his early teens he camped with the scouts every single Saturday, even when it was raining. On their trips, the scouts often carried only *onigiri*, rice rolled into the shape of a ball, triangle, or cylinder.

"He learned to appreciate a simple, modest life through the Boy Scout activities," Yuko said.

"And he learned how to cook at a camp of the Boy Scouts," Tadao said.

Kenji ascended to a leadership position within the scouts, and climbed nearby Mt. Fuji, the tallest mountain in Japan at 12,388 feet, as a sixth-grader.

When Kenji was in junior high, his parents allowed him to embark on a solo pilgrimage to thirty-four Buddhist temples in the Tokyo suburb of Chichibu. He walked fifty miles through pleasant countryside and green mountain paths, sleeping in garages and train sheds.

His independence grew as he got older, and he began to dream of going to college. A good student and an effective speaker, as well as the leader of a student association, Kenji had options when it came to higher education. His secret desire was to see the Southern Cross, a constellation not visible from most of Japan but noticeable on the horizon from the main island of Okinawa, the location of the University of the Ryukyus.

Driven by the chance to see the constellation and to get as far as he could from crowded Tokyo, Kenji applied to the university without telling his parents. The university accepted him, and he surprised his parents once more.

. . .

At their home in Tokyo, Kenji's parents recently thumbed through old photos. As they spotted a photo of five-year-old Kenji on the beach, they both remembered back to another time they realized their son was different from his brother, Masayuki, or any other child they knew.

Photo courtesy Kenji Yoshikawa

The family would sometimes travel to Tokyo Bay to dig for clams. The clamming was good one day, and Tadao, Yuko, and Masayuki were preoccupied with scraping at sand, pulling up clams, and plunking them in plastic buckets.

Young Kenji squinted as he looked up from the sand and scanned the broad estuary at the mouth of three rivers. He knew the big ocean was close, but he couldn't see it. The pull was irresistible.

He looked at his parents and brother, heads down at their diggings. He squinted around to memorize a few landmarks. Then, he headed toward the open ocean.

He figured he could walk until he saw the horizon of sea, and then come back before his parents missed him.

After a few minutes, Yuko looked up. She scanned the beach looking for her five-year-old.

"Tadao, where's Kenji!?" she said.

In a breathless panic, they rushed through soft sand to an aid station a good distance away. There Kenji was, so happy to see his parents that he blinked away tears. He had gone back to the spot at which his parents were clamming, but they were gone, sending lightning bolts of fear through him.

Strangely, the whole time Tadao and Yuko hugged Kenji, the attendant was laughing.

"What is so funny?" Tadao asked the man.

"Your son," the attendant said. "When he came up to me, instead of saying he was lost, like other children would, he said, 'Can you help me? My parents got lost.'"

Chapter Two

Fourth Rock from the Sun

From beneath his fur-lined hood, Tohru's smile is almost a laugh. Kenji, squinting at a problem, shakes his head. They are both near the metal grate steps of the Emmonak school, which are useful for shedding snow that has pillowed in Emmonak during the long subarctic winter. The white season began in October and cured when ice floes locked up the Yukon in November. A light snow is falling now, in this season of the sun's return, and the air temperature is two degrees Fahrenheit.

Kenji, who talked his way through the village grapevine of teacher, custodian, custodian's friend, has acquired from that friend, a local Native man, a long, red snowmachine sled made of ultra-high-molecular-weight polyethylene, a plastic that performs well in the cold. It is almost identical to the two sleds Kenji purchased months ago, the ones that are sitting in a warehouse in Anchorage, a place from which a shipping company can't guarantee they will budge anytime soon. Kenji has promised Jason, the man with the sled, a new one in return. It's a good deal for Jason, as the sleds are worth about $800 new. And it's a good deal for Kenji, because Jason's sled allows him to move. And he always wants to move.

With one hurdle cleared, now comes the execution of packing an expedition's worth of gear into one sled, and that is why Tohru is now laughing out loud. All the gear, piled on the sled, looks like a cleanup on aisle six waiting to happen. ActionPacker bins are stacked two stories high, and on top of their low-friction plastic lids are gun cases full of tools, black coils of tubing, and an orange bag containing an Arctic Oven tent. The load is tall, skinny, and chest-high.

"On the first turn, all that stuff's going to be on the tundra," Tohru says.

Kenji paces around the snowmachine and sled, surveying the load from different angles, imagining the bumps and curves of the trail. A few villagers have stopped to look at the load. The teenagers' faces, framed by cotton-hooded sweatshirts, remain blank, but one can imagine a smirk just beneath the surface.

Kenji motions to us to come over.

"Not going to work," he says, shaking his head.

This moment had to come, and I have been waiting for it. Though I have written a few times about Kenji's endeavors in Alaska, which catch my interest for their originality and degree of difficulty, my meetings with him have been brief. I don't really know what he's like on one of his expeditions.

Now I have a front-row seat as a problem surfaces, this one before a mile has clicked off his odometer. Is he a control freak who forces things to work even when they shouldn't, limping the operation along to fit a rigid plan, making everyone suffer in the process? Or is he like the hunting guide for whom I once worked, the guy who always promised his clients an animal, and always found a creative and usually legal way to get it done?

From looking at Kenji's life résumé—skiing to Antarctica, walking across the Sahara, sailing from Japan to Alaska—one would suspect he is the driven-but-flexible type. There seems no other way to complete these treks than to absorb the changes doled out by weather, to push through the creaks of a stressed body, and to shrug off the errors of others who don't care as much about your undertaking.

"Have to get the load down to one sled full," he says. "Let's bring everything back inside school."

Clunking up metal steps, we lug ten large ActionPacker totes back into the school, along with the tent, Kenji's drill box, his collection of drill bits in two weighty, conspicuous gun cases, tubes of PVC pipe twice as long as the ten-foot sled, and our bags of personal gear. Tohru and I, having anticipated a little more free time than has the man we'll be assisting, brought along our cross-country skis; they somehow made it to Emmonak strapped to a pallet when the giant sleds were left behind. Our skis and poles are among the first items Kenji recommends cutting, hinting that there will be little time for recreation on this trip.

"Tight schedule," he says.

Inside the carpeted entryway to the school, under Kenji's guidance, we further pare the load. A teacher at the school, a white man in his fifties who looks like he's logged many years of village time, stops by to shake Kenji's hand.

"Welcome to Emmonak," he says, yanking the bill of his baseball cap upward, so Kenji can see his eyes. "I've heard of you. Everybody's heard of the great Kan-gee."

Gil pulls from his jacket pocket a can of jarred salmon he harvested from somewhere near Anchorage, where—migrating between two worlds like a Canada goose—he spends his summers. He hands it to Kenji.

"Thank you," Kenji says, nodding.

Gil looks around at all our gear, winces, and issues a friendly warning.

"This is a third-world country," he says, his eyes darting down the hallways. "Watch your stuff."

A moment of uncomfortable silence follows. I try not to base judgments on a place on anybody else's opinion, but we have just arrived; Gil has worked and slept here for several years. I shoot a glance toward my backpack, which is leaning against a wall.

Gil is one of a few teachers we meet in Emmonak. The other, who seems to fit the same demographic, is Bill Sprott, a man from Delta Junction in Interior Alaska who came here three months ago to replace a teacher who left suddenly, reason undisclosed. Premature departures are not rare in Alaska villages, where students wound in the tentacles of parental alcoholism and other woes can eat up the unprepared. Teachers who have spent time in the Bush often say they have a hard time being accepted by some of the locals, even if they remain during their months of summer time off and pick salmon from nets alongside the villagers.

From my observations during our few hours here, perhaps influenced by Gil's comment, Emmonak seems a bit tougher than other villages. Because of frequent flooding in springtime due to ice jams that deflect the flow of water like sheets of plywood turned sideways, many of Emmonak's buildings hold the dark stains of the river. The houses, many constructed with government money (and of a standard frame design) have weathered many winters. Even the school, the most modern and expensive building in many villages, is dingy and dark.

But a visit in springtime is an unfair look at any place in Alaska, when many fine attributes are frozen, and one is distracted by dead snogos and pop cans and orange stains on the snow and chewed caribou hides.

Things are about to get tougher here. Emmonak is on the verge of a crisis, a recurring problem that many of rural Alaska's villages will share. The root of the trouble is the modern residue of the transition from dogteam to

snowmachine, from homemade mukluks to the days of daily plane service and lettuce from California.

Small communities like Emmonak are the early-warning system for the rest of Alaska, and perhaps the whole of the United States, because they run on gasoline and diesel and are the first to feel the effects of their scarcity and price fluctuations. Gasoline powers motorboats, snowmachines, four-wheelers, cars, trucks, and small aircraft; diesel warms houses and runs the rattling generators that provide electricity.

In its reliance on a substance extracted and refined in a place far away, Emmonak is similar to larger towns on the road system in Alaska. Despite the presence of an eight-hundred-mile-long, four-foot-diameter pipeline filled halfway to capacity and pushing oil across the state twenty-four hours a day, much of Alaska's fuel comes from refineries outside the state.

But there is one major difference between Alaska villages and places like Anchorage and Fairbanks on the road system: liquid fuel reaches Emmonak on slow-moving barges, which plug along in a sluggish race to visit all their customers before rivers and bays freeze in early fall.

Purchasers for the village, usually agents for Native corporations, pay the going rate for fuel when the barge arrives. This is like a lottery for people from

Emmonak; if the barge floats in while prices are relatively low, they win. In years like this one, they will lose, as the barge will be unable to penetrate ice at the mouth of the Yukon for the expected October delivery.

Instead, a fuel company will fly fuel in from Bethel later in the year. Even though diesel prices will have dropped by then from a drastic summer increase, the cost of flying in the weighty liquid jacked up gasoline prices to $7.25 per gallon. Heating oil, of which the average Emmonak household might need three fill-ups of a two-hundred-gallon tank during winter, costs $8.71 per gallon. At that rate, it would take about $2,000 to heat a small house, and that doesn't count the hike in electric bills that shadow the higher cost of diesel for the generators.

Fuel prices won't be Emmonak's only problem. In the coming year, the fish won't come back like they normally do in early June, at least not in numbers that would allow locals to sell them. Yukon River kings, especially those at the mouth of the river (where they are at their oiliest and most flavorful), were gaining a reputation as the new Copper River reds, favored by chic restaurants on the West Coast. Like the reds of a few decades earlier, Lower Yukon kings had gone from gillnet to ice to airplane to restaurant in less than a day. "It's the best fish in the sea, eating-wise," said Jon Rowley, a contributing editor to *Gourmet* who also manages communications for Kwik'pak Fisheries, the salmon-processing company in Emmonak. Rowley is the same man who introduced Copper River reds to the outside world in the 1980s.

"Yukon kings were just beginning to get a reputation as the ne plus ultra of fish, and the plug got pulled," he said in an interview with *Gourmet*'s Barry Estabrook.

Biologists for the Alaska Department of Fish and Game were the pullers of that plug. Trying to preserve the breeding stock of fish, the biologists made the tough call to cut subsistence fishing and close the commercial fishery after they looked at the numbers of fish entering the river at Emmonak and downstream.

As for the reason behind the scarcity of the Yukon's most important living resource, some people pointed fingers at the giant trawling ships dragging nets through the Bering Sea for pollock, a fish recognizable as the flaky white within fish sticks. More than one hundred of these trawlers crisscross the deep, fertile water off the mouth of the Yukon, and their nets by accident intercept kings bound for the big river. Pollock fishermen can't sell kings, so they dump them, usually dead, back into the Bering Sea. Whether the trawlers are responsible for the poor run of kings is not a sure thing; ocean temperatures, unusual mortality of Yukon salmon fry from the year before, and dozens of other subtle factors could

be part of the equation. But the reality of no chinook harvest hit Emmonak fisher-men like a wooden club. And more blows waited downstream.

After the nonexistent commercial fishing season and the airlifted fuel came a bitterly cold winter, which forced people in Emmonak to run their oil heaters on high for days on end. October, November, and January were colder than the hundred-year average at the weather station in Nome, the closest place monitored long term by the Alaska Climate Research Center. People also heat with wood, burning logs that were living trees hundreds of miles upriver, some falling in the river from cutbanks in Canada. But that resource, often plentiful and always appre-ciated, is not free. Villagers burn substantial amounts of gas sledding driftwood home by snowmachine and cutting it up with chainsaws. Fuel oil is the steadiest source of heat, made reliable by old drip heaters, in which the user adjusts the level himself, or thermostatically controlled units the size of a small dresser.

The trifecta of bad fortune—few fish, expensive fuel, and frigid air—inspired Emmonak resident Nicholas Tucker to send out a plea to the regional newspaper, the *Bristol Bay Times*. Tucker, a Native and lifelong resident of Emmonak, knew that winter was remarkable in its difficulty, so he got on his VHF radio and broad-cast a call asking how others were doing. He was surprised when more than a dozen people answered him. He visited the callers, had a cup of coffee with them at their kitchen tables, and jotted down their stories. He included each of their struggles in his letter to the *Times*, along with his own personal narrative.

My family of ten, with a household of six adults and four minors, is one of the casualties of our current high costs of heating fuel and gasoline that are devastating families and households here in Emmonak [which has] 847 residents. I am 63 and my wife is 54. For the first time, beginning December, I am forced to decide buying between heating fuel or groceries. I had been forced to dig into our January income to stay warm during December. Again, for this month, same thing happens. I am taking away my February income this month to survive. Couple of weeks ago, our 8-year old son had to go to bed hungry.

Sniffing an opportunity against former vice presidential candidate and Alaska Governor Sarah Palin, several Alaska bloggers picked up on Tucker's letter, which had appeared in an online version of the *Times*. The liberal-leaning writers posted it as an example of a politician more concerned with 2012 than with issues within her own state. With viral speed, Tucker's plea went nationwide, making its way into a story in the *Los Angeles Times*. Reporter Kim Murphy also quoted Dora Napoka, the librarian at the school in the village of Tuluksak, on the lower Kuskokwim River.

"Holy Jiminy Christmas, what we're going through," Napoka said. "It's like we have to choose between six gallons of stove oil or six gallons of gas to go out and get the firewood—or does my baby need infant milk? Which one is more important?"

The words of despair, from a soft-spoken people, caught the attention of people who don't live in Native villages, at least temporarily. Churches and other relief groups sent food to Emmonak and to other villages, and elders in Emmonak received vouchers for free fuel. The Bureau of Indian Affairs sent an infusion of $20,000 in emergency cash to Emmonak villagers to help pay for food and fuel. Sarah Palin traveled with a Christian group called Samaritan's Purse to deliver food to residents of two other Lower Yukon River villages, Marshall and Russian Mission.

Tucker traveled by snowmachine to Russian Mission to visit the governor, getting about four minutes of face-to-face conversation in a crowded gymnasium. He later reported that he was less than satisfied with the governor's response—that people in the villages could also work outside the villages, as her husband Todd did once, splitting time between Dillingham and oil work on the North Slope.

There seem to be no easy answers to the village fuel problems, but several groups of people within villages have revived or created new projects to erect turbines to harness a plentiful resource, wind. (Wales, on the tip of the Seward Peninsula that points toward Russia, has an average wind speed of eighteen miles per hour.) Tanana residents have installed a large wood-fired boiler system. Researchers at the University of Alaska Fairbanks are looking at the viability of large, screw-type devices submerged in large rivers to provide power as the blade turns. Scientists are also applying for grants to study the potential of geothermal power from seismic hot spots, an idea that had stalled for decades because of cheap and subsidized fuel. And people in Galena are thinking again of the offer from a Japanese company to install a small nuclear reactor that could power the whole village, at little cost to the villagers—if you don't count the risk of what might happen during a major earthquake.

· · ·

Out on the edge of Emmonak, where, like a pre-Columbian sailor you might assume the world was flat because the great delta is a tabletop of blown snow, Ron steps off his Polaris snowmachine.

"Kotlik's this way," he says, pointing to a snowmachine trail that trends northeast until willow brush swallows it.

Over a gray hooded sweatshirt, Ron, a white man of about fifty who married a local woman years ago, wears a black leather jacket. Ron has stringy blond hair, bad teeth, and ten kids, including Little Ron, whom we met at the school. Little Ron, a raven-haired ten-year-old, was more interested in talking with us than in listening to his teachers, which earned him two trips to the principal.

Rather than a hat or snowmachine helmet, Ron Sr. wears cup-type industrial hearing protectors over his sweatshirt hood, which seems to be a style unique to the Lower Yukon. Back at the school, Ron saw us sorting our stuff and, with Little Ron weaving among us and asking questions, hung around to chat. He mentioned he had just returned from winter gathering of driftwood.

"I get wood from my fish camp, about thirty miles upriver," Ron said.

Kenji stopped taping data cables together and looked up at Ron. Kenji is unfailingly polite, but there are some people to whom he listens with more concentration. Ron is someone who travels the ground in and out of the village everyday, and knows the landscape like you know the streets of your hometown. These people are gold to Kenji, because many crooked fingers of trail lead out of each village.

If you were to guess which way it was from Emmonak to the closest village of Kotlik, and if you were born with an exceptional sense of direction, you might choose the trail to Kotlik about 60 percent of the time. But, as Kenji learned in Australia and the dripping Amazon and the foggy small boat harbor at Nome, it is much more efficient to humbly ask directions than to boldly strike out and twenty minutes later end up at someone's fish camp.

In the school, Kenji asked Ron, "Will you show us the way out of town?"

Pleased, Ron nodded. "I'll be by to get you tomorrow."

On the fringe of Emmonak, Ron lifts one cup off his ear to speak with Kenji.

"You head this way," he says, pointing to a maze of blank white and neck-high willows. "You'll find other trails merging from the south; then, you'll be on a staked trail to Kotlik, with some tripods and some wood stakes. Look for green markers on the stakes."

"Thank you, thank you," Kenji says, shaking Ron's gloved hand with both of his.

Kenji, dressed entirely in black, is wearing insulated coveralls over which he pulled a down parka with a ruff of polar bear fur he acquired in Barrow, rubber boots that are not as well insulated as his warmer boots in the warehouse with the sleds in Anchorage, and a set of goggles, to which he has glued fur to the inverted U of the nose bridge. He looks like Groucho Marx, but cold air won't kill any of the skin cells on his nose today. Kenji has already donated that tissue in the name of learning, when he lived in an igloo in the Canadian Arctic, shuffled his feet across Greenland, and leaned into the winds at the South Pole.

Our destination for the night is a classroom floor in the village of Stebbins, about 105 miles from Emmonak. But Kenji first wants to stop about halfway in Kotlik, a village about the same size as Emmonak (with even higher fuel prices). There, he hopes to meet with the science teacher and drill a permafrost observatory similar to the one he drilled in Emmonak. And he wants to do it in an hour or less. The Yoshikawa Hit-and-Run.

Ron's directions will save a good deal of daylight. The way is not obvious out here. Unfold a map of this country and you are looking at Swiss cheese. Aside from swamp symbols and dark blue lakes, which are often indistinguishable from land in winter, there are no landmarks whatsoever, on either the maps or the horizon in front of us, at least to my eye.

If not useful for navigation, the USGS map is interesting in a historical sense. On it are the ghost towns of Hamilton, New Hamilton, Naguchik, and Bill Moores. A cluster of black rectangles represents each place. These were cabins when mapmakers drew them in the 1950s, and a few fish camps—frame structures draped with ribbons of blue tarp—are still around and look usable. But most of those names on the map no longer exist, even out here, where the subfreezing temperatures that persist for seven months of each year disable the tiny organisms that gobble wood, metal, leather, and plastic in the steady process of decomposition.

A person might depend on the maps for general direction of travel, but Kenji will probably not pull one out today. He will instead rely on the trail markers to get us to Kotlik, and with his peripheral vision will sense the sun's position to confirm we're going the right way.

He has adjusted to the shipping company's mistake by further trimming our load so that most of it fits in the red sled, with our personal bags behind the seats of our three snowmachines. We now carry six ActionPackers instead of ten, and the outfit no longer resembles a double-decker bus. Now it's knee-high and ratcheted down with so many nylon straps that the sled would have to disintegrate for anything to spill on the tundra.

Kenji the scientist made some hard choices in deciding what to cut back, leaving behind the bulk of his accessories for drilling permafrost observatories. Bill Sprott

has agreed to ship our leftover gear to Unalakleet, which we hope will meet the rest of Kenji's original shipment from Anchorage and become a complete unit.

The man in black has adapted, and, like he was on the hot night in Algeria on the eve of his first step across the Sahara, he is so excited to see new country that the feeling overpowers the three hours of sleep he had on the floor of the Yupik language teacher's classroom.

Before moving, though, Kenji and Tohru pose for a photo by Tohru's machine, the one attached to the sled. Kenji will lead, and I will take up the rear and pick up any items that escape the bonds of the sled.

"You ready?" Kenji asks.

Barely able to hear him through my own beaver-fur cap, borrowed from a friend who made it while teaching in a village, I give him the thumb's up. Tohru nods. Ron lifts a gloved hand and, looking a bit sad not to be joining us, peels off toward the village.

We are one hundred miles from the nearest living spruce tree, about to embark on a journey to the Arctic Circle by tracing the nose of the Seward Peninsula with snowmachine tracks. Into a bending horizon of neon blue, with a tripod of leaning spruce stems providing the only break from a flat world poked with naked twigs, we start up our machines. One after the other, we flex our right thumbs, our tracks break free of ice, and we pull away from Emmonak.

■ ■ ■

July 21, 1976, was a sultry day in Tokyo: an eighty-five-degree afternoon when people wished the monsoon approaching from the southwest would just go ahead and soak them. Kenji, then thirteen, had just returned from a Boy Scout trip to nearby hills, and was contemplating how he could make his backpack lighter the following week.

Forty-eight million miles away, a manmade object was falling toward the fourth planet from the sun. Just as a few dozen anxious men in Texas had planned, a vessel that looked like a flying saucer separated from its propulsion vehicle. Slowed by a parachute that stalled its descent through a thin carbon-dioxide atmosphere, the saucer birthed a landing craft that resembled a spider with four legs.

Firing its engines, the lander wafted down to the reddish surface of Mars. Upon its touchdown, men in shirts, ties, and glasses rimmed with black plastic hugged each other in a control room in Houston. For the first time, Americans had set a mechanical foot on the Red Planet.

Photo courtesy Mary A. Dale-Bannister, Washington University in St. Louis

Those engineers and programmers then radioed instructions to the lander to take a photograph of one of its own feet, standing on the surface of Mars. Not only did such an image prove that the lander was where they thought it was, it would allow them to see how much the craft penetrated the surface. The competing Russians had a notion that Mars had the texture of quicksand, but the craft sunk no more than it would have on a Texas lawn.

The first image transmitted from Mars was a black-and-white shot of the disc of an orbiter's foot resting atop a surface that resembled a drained lakebed, with rocks poking through a sandy surface. During the following months, the camera took color photos of the surface of Mars. With a little imagination, the viewer could be looking at the desert near Sedona, Arizona. Mars had gullies, the tracks of dust devils etched into its surface, polygons similar to those formed by ice on Alaska's North Slope, sand dunes, and castles of orange rock. Other features, like the dark craters with no apparent bottom, were not so much like Earth.

After the Viking lander touched down, Tadao Yoshikawa set a copy of the daily *Yomiuri Shimbun* on the kitchen table as he returned home from work. Kenji, always eager to see the paper, picked it up. He saw an image of an exotic orange landscape on the front page.

"Dad, look," he said. "They have a picture of Mars!"

Kenji stared at the rocks and the hills that looked so climbable, almost like a landscape on Earth. His mind drifted from the familiar to the absurd. What if someone lived there?

At that moment, staring at that desertlike landscape, Kenji made a few silent vows. First, if the far-out opportunity ever presented itself, he would go to Mars. Second, he would prepare himself for that remote possibility by getting to know his own planet. Not by reading books, though he would do that too, but by traveling to deserts and ice caps and jungles and oceans and mountains. He wanted to be able to open his world atlas to any page and have an image pop up in his mind, one he put there himself.

"If I know about Earth," the thirteen-year-old boy reasoned, "I can tell a Martian about our planet."

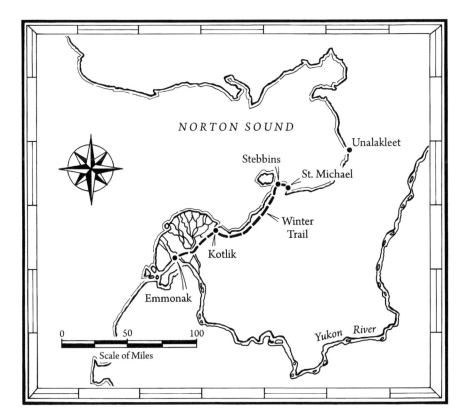

Chapter Three

Wretched Little Port

To anyone else the wretched little port of St. Michael on the Bering Sea, with its melancholy mud flats, its grey warehouses, its rusty Russian cannon, and its stink of rotting fish, might have seemed to be the end of the earth. But to the prospectors it was Utopia.

—Pierre Berton, *Klondike*

In fall of 1897, eighteen hundred gold stampeders paused here, chattering with excitement as they tried to envision their upcoming river trip to Dawson City in the Yukon Territory. Dawson, everyone knew, was the place with the gold in its creeks, weighty nuggets that would change their lives.

The argonauts of a century ago who passed through St. Michael were taking what Canadian historian Pierre Berton called "the rich man's route" to the gold-fields. Gold seekers who had the cash could book passage on a ship and travel three thousand miles from Seattle to St. Michael (via Dutch Harbor), and then board a sternwheeler for the seventeen-hundred-mile trip to Dawson City. Compared to lugging sacks of beans and flour up Chilkoot Pass or trying to pull a boat up the cold boil of the Copper River, the St. Michael route was a cinch.

"In theory," Berton wrote, "no one needed to walk a foot of the distance: it was a boat ride all the way."

While the desperate, hopeful, adventurous people on this route would indeed make it to Dawson by ship, the trips dragged out for months longer than they imagined. The stampeders who didn't go nuts were the patient, a virtue shared by perhaps all the successful pick-and-shovel miners throughout history—those who mucked out gravels all winter by thawing frozen soils with fires, and then waited months to sift through the tailings.

Though most of the hopeful came back with nothing but stories, there was indeed gold in the Klondike, and a few early prospectors found incredible wealth in

Dawson City. St. Michael welcomed the lucky ones who would later start the stampede to the Klondike by arriving in Seattle on steamships listing with gold. Berton described the eighty or so passengers who came down the Yukon and out to St. Michael on the steamers *Portus B. Weare* and *Alice*: "There was gold in suitcases and leather grips, gold in boxes and packing-cases, gold in belts and pokes of caribou hide, gold in jam jars, medicine bottles, and tomato cans, and gold in blankets held by straps and cord, so heavy it took two men to hoist each one aboard."

The prospectors had the wealth of their dreams pressing down the decks, but it hadn't bought them the tang of a peach. "As each vessel in turn puffed out of the labyrinth of the Yukon delta and headed up the somber coastline to the volcanic island on which the port was perched, a wave of excitement rippled among the passengers. For there was food at St. Michael, and an orgy followed each landing. It was fruit and vegetables the miners wanted, and they devoured tins of pineapple, apricots, and cherries, swilled cider at a dollar a bottle, and gnawed away on raw turnips."

St. Michael fired the salivary glands of the stampeders, most of whom knew they would never return to these tundra hills humming with mosquitoes. But St. Michael didn't ghost out after the gold seekers left, making it different than Iditarod, Flat, Suntrana, Star City, Nation, Caribou Bar, Caro, Liberty, Jack Wade, Dall City, Placerville, Poorman, Cripple, Long, Dime Landing, Haycock, Solomon, Lost River, Bonanza, Nizina, Sumdum, Comet, Porcupine, Georgetown, Dyea, Wortmanns, Franklin, Ivy City, Independence, and Seventymile, among others.

Unlike those transient towns, St. Michael was not a product of the gold rush, predating it by more than half a century. To exploit the trade opportunities and ample cash to be made off furs, the Russians, with their capital of New Archangel (Sitka) in eastern Alaska, wanted a base in western Alaska, ideally a deep-water bay close to the mouth of the Yukon and also near Native traders at Golovnin Bay on the Seward Peninsula.

St. Michael, then known as Mikhailovskii, was that port. It would become a city of American dreams and then shrivel to one of the smallest Eskimo villages in western Alaska. One wonders if there are still a few grains of gold dust on its bleak volcanic beach or within the clumps of tussock tundra that surround the village. Like the one into which Kenji will soon sink his drill.

. . .

At the end of a long Kenji day, it's five below zero in St. Michael. The slight heat of the day has fled with the sun, which is tucked behind afternoon clouds in the

direction of Stebbins, the other village on the island. Though it's hard to imagine this place as anything other than a gritty village on the wane, twenty thousand people stepped on this frozen soil during 1897 and 1898, when St. Michael was the construction center for thirty steamboat companies. That's when the town featured the Hotel Healy, which could host five hundred guests at once. If the structure still stood, which it doesn't, it could accommodate the current residents of St. Michael with fifty rooms left over.

Today, St. Michael is quiet, except for the screams of a raven sitting on the town's 1.2-million-gallon water tank, a few stories high and coated with spray foam that the sun has ripened to a deep orange. There's also the hum of a small generator that Kenji uses to power his electric drill, the most important tool in his sliding caravan.

At eight o'clock on this late winter evening, he is drilling again. It's the second hole Kenji will poke into St. Michael Island today. And, though we're on an island, you wouldn't recognize it as such even if you were flying over. A canal dredged by the U.S. Army Corps of Engineers in about 1910 separates the landmass from the mainland. The corps mucked out the fifteen-mile slough so that shallow-draft steamboats could avoid the stretch of open ocean near Stebbins (then Atuik), at the northwest corner of St. Michael Island. This fifty-five-square-mile mass of volcanic rock takes up about as much space as Minneapolis, though the population density here is sixteen people per square mile, compared to the sixty-seven hundred souls pressing down on the same amount of ground in Minneapolis.

As far as we can tell, we three are the only ones moving in this part of the village, near the plywood-covered frame of a new school. Tohru, at Kenji's side, cradles a handheld blowtorch within his parka, trying to influence its small propane tank with his body heat. He wants to warm a metal drilling shaft to above the freezing point.

"I don't know what's colder—this torch or me," Tohru says.

Kenji says nothing, leaning into his drill. He grunts with effort. The drill groans to a halt.

"Stuck again."

Kenji is drilling a hole in the tundra and soil using a drill bit that he fabricated in his garage. He got the idea for the arrowhead-shape tip from characters in a Saturday-morning cartoon. While watching with his children as *Speed Racer* gouged a hole to the center of the Earth, Kenji grabbed a pen and sketched the bit on an envelope. He thought the shape would be perfect for chewing through frozen soil. It does a pretty good job.

Because his task of drilling frozen ground while on the fly is so unique, Kenji gathered or invented his own system: a fifty-five-pound Honda generator, a forty-pound Bosch electric drill, a smaller drill for his narrow "frost tube" holes, and drill bits he designed for different mediums—silt, gravel, and bedrock. He also carries lightweight shafts made for sea ice; they work in frozen silt and other rockless soils.

Each steel drill shaft is two inches in diameter and as tall as Kenji's waist. When he penetrates frozen soil to the length of the shaft, he yanks it out of the hole, removes the shaft from the chuck, and joins another shaft to it after Tohru hands it to him. In this fashion, Kenji penetrates the ground beneath our feet with twenty feet of connected shafts. Gaining that length—by joining three-foot shaft to three-foot shaft, drilling down another few feet and attaching another one—is the challenging part in cold weather. Below about ten degrees Fahrenheit, his shafts tend to stick together, or don't want to mate at all.

With his bare hand wrapped around the shaft (which is so cold it should burn like a red-hot pipe, though Kenji doesn't flinch), he uses a hammer to tap a pin that connects both sections of threaded shaft. The cold adds time to this endeavor, as it did this morning in Stebbins. There, twenty miles away, past the

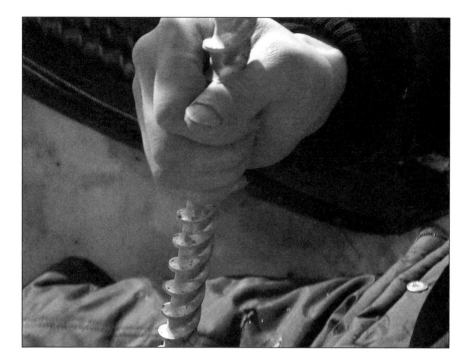

ancient eruption cones that are the island's hills and the circular, clear lakes that are the water supplies for both villages, Kenji had a busy morning.

After waking on the classroom floor, Kenji got dressed and drove the snow-machine out on the sea ice west of Stebbins. There, bathed in the pink light of sunrise, Kenji drilled a plug of sea ice that he would save for a professor at the university in Fairbanks who studies that ephemeral substance.

Less than an hour later, Kenji met with a class of students at a site behind the Stebbins school, where the night before he had shoved a plastic tube filled with blue water into the ground. This "frost tube" allows students to follow the freezing front as the northern part of the globe tilts toward darkness and cold slowly and thoroughly soaks into the ground. The frost can permeate dozens of feet during a year without much snow, which helps insulate the surface from bitter air.

After giving the students a classroom lecture, Kenji found a spot out by a power pole to drill his first permafrost observatory of the day. There, as the rising sun exploded into sundogs behind him, he willed his way through stuck drill bits and frozen soil. He finished with a fifteen-foot hole into which he slipped a cable with sensors spaced a few feet apart so he could take the temperature of the ground at different levels.

In Stebbins permafrost, a typical profile in summertime would be—regard-less of the air temperature at eye level—about thirty-one degrees at the tempera-ture sensors three, six, nine, and fifteen feet below the ground surface. Stebbins has warmish permafrost that will thaw if air temperatures climb and remain high. As in much of Alaska, the air in summer has been warmer than the historical aver-age in Stebbins since about the mid-1970s.

No permafrost is in danger on this late winter day in St. Michael. It's so cold that the metal shaft has fused with the earth it had briefly thawed. The stuck rod is another small problem in a day that began with one, when Kenji needed to find someone in Stebbins to spot-weld one of his shafts. He found someone, as Kenji always does, and got his welding done.

With a bit of grimacing, some cursing in Japanese, and many watts of muscle power, Kenji wrenches his equipment free. He backs the shaft out of the hole, which erupts in coffee-ground chunks of frozen soil.

"Get ready," he says to Tohru.

Anticipating Kenji's needs, Tohru shoves two-inch-diameter PVC pipe into the hole before it collapses on itself. He then snakes in wires that reach to the bottom of the hole and plugs the wires into a matchbook-size datalogger. The setup will allow Kenji, when he rides back to check temperatures tomorrow, to at least get the temperature of St. Michael's permafrost right now, should anything happen to his equipment. And random vandalism is not beyond the realm of possibility, since Kenji has covered his work with a metal Folger's can (due to the fact that the PVC pipe that is still in an Anchorage warehouse). The can sits in the snow, a shiny red bull's-eye.

When we pack up the drill bits, the sun has set, and it is ten p.m., still light enough to read a book outside as the subarctic approaches springtime—if one doesn't mind reading at ten below zero.

We ride our snowmachines back to the school, using the key the teacher gave us to enter his science class. After eating a few microwave burritos in the school kitchen, we pile back into the classroom and onto our sleeping mats for the night. The classroom floor is not clean, with bits of paper, staples, soil, and unidentified objects on the carpet, but we are so exhausted after this typical Kenji day that we don't care.

Snores fill the room as the temperature drops outside. A weather station we have set outside on a snowmachine tells us the temperature during the night drops to twenty-three below. Heating oil sucked from the ground in Canada, refined in California, boated to Anchorage, and then barged to St. Michael keeps the classroom in the high seventies.

After a bad night's sleep on the classroom floor, we get up early and pack our things before the kids get to class at seven. We pile our bags in the narrow hallway amid dark-haired children in basketball jerseys with iPod buds in their ears. The school is old, dark, and has few windows. Though this last feature saves energy, the lack of natural light probably takes its toll on the morale of teachers and the enthusiasm of students.

■ ■ ■

We have sixty miles to travel today by snowmachine. These miles will be much more challenging than the distance we have traveled from Emmonak to St. Michael. There is a packed trail out of St. Michael for thirty-five miles, as far as the Golsovia River, where former Iditarod musher Jerry Austin runs a lodge catering to tourists who want a dog-mushing adventure. But Kenji, with Tohru and me following, will be breaking trail the remaining few hours into Unalakleet. You could forgive any traveler for hitting the trail as early as possible, but Kenji lingers in a dreary classroom, speaking to seven students, executing a part of his mission that is as important to him as the science.

A few years ago, when science "outreach activities" became mandatory hurdles on the track to government funds, Kenji's boss suggested he drill a permafrost borehole at Pearl Creek Elementary School in Fairbanks.

With his heavy Japanese accent, Kenji knows that people sometimes have trouble understanding him. He remedied that by taking the Pearl Creek students out in the woods, where they helped him while he was drilling. He made them laugh as they assisted him, even though they didn't understand all his words.

He found that he loved outreach, and envisioned it as a large part of his new adventures in Alaska. Tohru, it turned out, knew a teacher in the northwest Alaska village of Noatak. Kenji visited there, felt a kinship with the Bush children in the classroom and their resource-strapped teachers, and repeated his Pearl Creek experience. He was hooked.

"Once I started, I think it was no fair to stop," Kenji says. "I have to go to other villages, to all the villages. That's my character—all or nothing. Something between is bad."

In the St. Michael classroom, he starts by asking the kids their names. "Michael, OK," he says. He draws "Michael" on the board in Japanese characters. "You? Cyrus? OK . . . You? Agnes? OK." The kids giggle as they see their names as symbols. Some copy them in their notebooks.

"You hear lots about global warming, news and TV," Kenji says, gesturing with his arms in a gray canvas shirt beneath suspenders, wearing an Under Armour black cap over the bullet of his bald head. "But do you feel anything about global warming? Something changing? Is barge coming in much earlier? Middle of winter, still ocean doesn't freeze?"

Cyrus, a tired-looking boy wearing a camouflage cap, raises his hand.

"Feels like it's getting colder," he says.

Kenji nods.

"You can get information from movie, from TV, from newspaper, but also you have to figure out by yourself—is [global warming] true or not? Everybody in the world could say true, but if you feel [it's] not, it's OK. That's why I'm asking.

"This year cold, next year maybe warmer. Some years colder, some years warmer, that's a cycle. Longer trend, fifty or one hundred years, going to be warmer or colder? That's what we are talking about.

"We drill a permafrost hole here, to see how frozen soil is," Kenji says. "Then we can get temperatures right now for the permafrost in this area, which we can compare to later to see if it got warmer, or maybe colder.

"Maybe, in fifty years when you are elder and I will maybe be gone, then you can remember this permafrost hole and go back and check to see what temperatures have done. Maybe you have a grandchild, and you can tell them, 'I know where to measure the temperature of the ground.' This will be the real value of this research."

With a typhoon approaching Okinawa, Kenji removes his first sailboat from the water near the village of Yomitan. Photo courtesy Kenji Yoshikawa.

Chapter Four

Empty Spots

B reezes that caress your skin with warmth, even on the shortest day of winter. White coral beaches lapped by clear, aquamarine water. Locals who—because of good genes, healthy food, and a gentle environment—often breathe island air for a century (with an average life expectancy of 81.2 years, one of the longest in the world). Sugar cane, hibiscus flowers, bananas, and papayas growing in backyards. In the air, the clean tang of the sea.

The Ryukyu Islands are the subtropical paradise of Japan, a land without winter, where water tanks sit on roofs with no threat of icing, a place where the human animal could survive most of the year without clothing.

Arcing southward from the large islands of Japan to the Tropic of Cancer, the Ryukyus are closer to Taiwan than to Tokyo. That distance is what attracted Kenji to Okinawa: it was the farthest south he could wander and still be in Japan.

In Okinawa, the eighteen-year-old Kenji was liberated from his parents for the first time. For such an adventurous person, this freedom had its dangers, but another of Kenji's traits, somewhat unusual for someone with his curiosity and ability, is how he seeks out those who have trodden similar ground before he shoulders his way into it.

Sensing a kindred soul, he sought out a professor at the university who was known for his travels to Antarctica and the Himalayas, performing cold-weather science, climbing big mountains, and earning the respect of both mountaineers and his peer scientists.

Kohshiro Kizaki

Kohshiro Kizaki, now in his mid-eighties, lives in Shuri, the ancient capital of Okinawa, the largest island of the Ryukyus. Kizaki, a happy man with an expressive face, saw in Kenji a younger reflection of himself. "Out of the blue, without any information, he came to see me," Kizaki remembered on a humid fall day in his office in Shuri, a busy but pleasant district of the city of Naha. He sat at a table, drinking coffee, surrounded by his painting—realist works of the South Pole, magnified ice crystals, and a pastel street scene in a French village.

Okinawans have a certain mind-set, Kizaki says, and Kenji was a pleasant contrast to many of the young students. "The Okinawa prefecture consists of forty or fifty small islands," he explained. "Every island has its own dialect and each dialect is quite different from one another. The Okinawa Island is the biggest one, and, how shall I put it, people are strongly connected—they have a strong identity, and their identity is directed inward. Students at [Ryukyu] university, especially those from the local area, didn't try everything, didn't like going outside, even to the main island [of Japan] to get a job. They liked to stay here, marry, and have a house."

Kenji banded with a few like-minded students in Okinawa, "who would do something new, something unusual—they had a sort of outlaw spirit," said Kizaki. "Kenji is quite different. He is physically very strong. That's one thing," he says. "Another thing is he stresses his idea. His idea, his dream, is to go to Mars, into the universe."

■ ■ ■

Okinawa, Kenji's favorite place he has lived so far, shaped his mind and his body. Already blessed with uncommon power and trained in aikido and judo during his middle- and high-school years, he saw a group of muscled young men running each morning before the sun rose over the island. A friend told him they were boxers, working with Okinawa boxing coach Shoei Uehara.

Uehara, a concrete block of a man with thick hands, was a trainer of several world-champion boxers, among them Yoko Gushiken, World Boxing Association light flyweight champion from 1976 to 1981.

Uehara and his wife, Miyoko, ran a boxing gym, and they helped Uehara's brother operate a public bath. Uehara required his young boxers to polish the floor in the bathhouse, using a circular motion with their nondominant hand. Uehara also directed his boxers to sprint up the crowded streets of Naha, the largest city on Okinawa, when people were just getting out of work. Their task—to weave amid the flow of people without touching anyone. To teach boxers to keep their arms in, Uehara made them clamp 10,000 yen ($100) notes within their armpits during workouts without dropping them. He also encouraged some boxers, including Kenji, to take up ballroom dancing to improve their footwork.

When young Kenji showed up at the door of Uehara's gym, the coach ran his eyes over him and marveled at his luck. "Kenji had a great body, and he was trained in judo, so I thought he could be a world champion," Uehara said over a dinner of broiled pig's feet in a wood-paneled bar, its open doorway ushering in the delicious warm air of an Okinawa October night. "He is also patient, and that's why we became friends. If he had lost his temper easily, we wouldn't have. He was always cheerful."

Kenji became Uehara's prize student, and a surrogate member of the Uehara family. He trained with the coach, ate healthy meals prepared by Miyoko, and played with and tutored their children. Uehara trained him for free. He saw in Kenji a younger version of himself, with a passion for adventure that he had for boxing.

Miyoko and Shoei Uehara with Kenji

Miyoko says she found Kenji to be an inspiring model on how to live. "He is very skillful at making his way through life," she said. "He can get along well with anyone, and he is not fussy about what he eats.

"I think twenty-four hours a day were not enough for Kenji," she said. "He used twenty-four hours efficiently—helping kids at an after-school study group, working as a security guard, studying at the university. He'd sleep whenever he had a little time, and then would get up and go to the next activity. Watching him work that way, I always thought I'd have to use my time efficiently; otherwise I'd end up wasting my life. He valued every minute.

"Kenji came to Okinawa not only to study but also to bring himself closer to his dream," she said. "I think adventure was his dream. He didn't derail from it. He made his way for it."

The Okinawa boxing gym was the sun that Kenji orbited—up at five for a run, attend some college classes until early afternoon, back to the gym for work on the speed-bag and a bit of sparring. After that, he cleaned up the gym and went over the Ueharas' home for dinner. After finishing, he'd tutor their children for a few hours, and then return to his dorm. With his remaining brainpower, he'd slip in a bit of college homework before going to a local hotel, where he worked at the front desk.

His life was similar to the hardworking days and nights of any up-and-coming professional boxer. The dream suited his talents. Everything was in place: a motivated, talented athlete paired with a coach who had molded world champions and was hungry for another.

But life soon deviated from the script. One afternoon, when Kenji entered the gym, Uehara motioned him over. Kenji had never seen his mentor so distraught; he expected news of a death.

"I've lost it," Uehara said, running his large hands through his thinning hair.

"You've lost what?" Kenji said.

"Everything," Uehara said. "The gym. The bathhouse. Everything."

"What happened?" Kenji said.

Almost in tears, Uehara told Kenji of how he had been a guarantor for a friend who defaulted on a loan. Knowing how kind-hearted Uehara was, Kenji wasn't surprised at how events unfolded.

"Now, we will lose both the gym and the bathhouse," Uehara said. "We are finished."

The next day, the door on the gym was locked, and the reality of the new situation descended upon Kenji. His daily routine changed—no more boxing, no more world-championship dreams—he couldn't imagine them without Uehara and his life at the gym.

Though he still ate dinner with the Ueharas and tutored their two boys and two girls, he found his mind drifting back to a dream born in his boyhood classrooms, where he would leave his world atlas open to the map of Australia, stealing peeks while the teacher was speaking of something else. He hummed the traditional song "Tsuki No Sabaku" (Moon over the Desert), which captivated young Kenji as he dreamed of oasis palm trees and camels. The great deserts there were his first goal.

"I had zero idea of what [the deserts of Australia] looked like," he says. "Why was it empty? Why didn't the map say much? I'd like to see why this was empty. I want to see empty spots."

He had another reason he was fascinated with the desert.

"In Japan, where it's so humid, many people have a passion about the desert," Kenji says. "Mars, to me, looked like the desert. I feel like I can't go Mars, but I can go to desert, maybe feel like Mars."

■ ■ ■

As soon as Kenji turned twenty, he applied for a ticket to freedom, his passport. As an undergraduate, he had no money for the Australia trip, but he did have a means, a Bridgestone bike. It would carry him across a swath of planet too hot for human settlement.

He worked nights at the front desk of an Okinawa hotel, and, though it shorted his sleep, he saved enough for a plane ticket to Darwin, in Australia's Northern Territory.

He reassembled his bike in Darwin, and started on a journey to Adelaide, about two thousand miles away in South Australia. He felt the same thrill of a decade earlier, when he rode across Tokyo to his cousin's house. Only this time he knew no one along the way. And the country was exotic to him. Once he got away from the coast and into the arid zone, his lips began chapping in the dry air. He let them crack, and drank in the sharp accents of the people as he tried to understand them, the stringy brush somehow sustained by the dry soil, the omnipresent sun, the strangeness of it all.

He pedaled through desert country on unpaved roads, about one hundred miles each day. He camped under bridges and became skilled at replacing spokes that buckled from the bumps of washboard roads. He saved sand in plastic bags and weighed down his bike with them because he wanted to know the composition of minerals that created the great deserts (he would later write a report on his conclusions for the university). He carried in jugs about three gallons of water, which he would refill whenever he reached a village. His budget was about five

Photo courtesy Kenji Yoshikawa

dollars per day, which led to a Spartan diet—water, juice, a bit of corned beef for dinner, plus a staple that was his only meal when he ran out of everything else.

"In general, just eat bread," he says.

One day, as he spun out on soft sand and broke another spoke, he felt like quitting. Who cared anyway? He was just a young guy in the desert, on a mission that was important to him alone. As he was sitting there, he contemplated throwing his bike in the bushes and hitchhiking out of there. He resisted the urge to chuck it all, and took a few breaths.

As he was sitting there, a dragonfly spun crazily down and landed on his knee. He noticed it had a broken wing, and would die soon. But the dragonfly groomed its head with its front legs as if it was perfectly content. It then flew from his knee to his bike.

"When I see him, looking so happy, I think, Why should I give up?" Kenji says.

Kenji fixed his spoke and continued on, the dragonfly clinging to his bike for more than an hour before it cartwheeled off into the breeze.

Kenji loved meeting people along the road, the spring sun on his skin, and how sleeping under the stars each night recharged him. He learned a few things on his month-and-a-half adventure: pack a lot of extra spokes, you can't drink too much water in the desert, avoid riding at midday if you can, and ask questions of everyone.

Photo courtesy Kenji Yoshikawa

Near the end of his trip, thirty days after he started, Kenji reached Port Augusta on the Southern Ocean. He knew the cool breeze that poured over him was coming from another mystery, Antarctica. He started thinking about his Australia trip, and his goals for the future.

"I was bit disappointed because there were bushes," he says. "And I never saw dunes, typical desert . . . I had tons of time while biking to think of Sahara."

Before he had drawn a red line across Australia on the Michelin world map he kept on his wall, Kenji made plans to see the landscape he envisioned as a boy. He wanted to cross the world's iconic desert. On foot this time.

■ ■ ■

Less than a year after his Australia trip, Kenji again took a few more semesters off from college, this time to visit the greatest desert in the world. He had even less money than he had saved for the Australia trip, but was confident he could lean out his needs to make the trip. His goal was to spend one dollar per day.

In part to prepare for the trip and in part because he wanted to, Kenji walked from the southern tip of the island of Kyushu to Tokyo, carrying nothing but a towel and a few hundred yen (a few dollars). He slept under bridges, ate up thirty-plus miles each day, and got a great tan. And, he once again surprised his parents when he walked into the house when they didn't expect him. He told them of his plans for the Sahara. They were mildly shocked—it was the Sahara, after all—but they weren't surprised. They were growing accustomed to the fact that something big would always be on Kenji's horizon.

Kenji had envisioned another solo journey, across the red dunes of the Sahara, but heard of a guy from Osaka, three years older than himself, who had almost exactly the same plan.

Eiji Yamamoto had a dream of walking across the planet. Like Kenji, Yamamoto wanted to traverse the Sahara. By chance, he had chosen exactly the same route—from Laghouat, Algeria, to deep into Niger—and the same winter to complete the trek.

Kenji met Eiji through other members of an adventure cycling club to which they both belonged. Though each man planned to travel alone—and was looking forward to the solitude—Eiji called Kenji to share the simple camaraderie of discussing their trips. While they spoke, remembering the loneliness of his Australia trip, Kenji pondered traveling with a stranger. Since they had planned identical journies, at the same time, Kenji thought they were fated to go together. Years later, he sees the Sahara trip as the start of something good.

"If you're solo, it's good, but you can't share experience," he says. "To go together is fun, to share memory later—it's one of the most beautiful things. If you go with somebody, share, that makes happiness."

. . .

The travelers were soon in Laghouat, Algeria, at the base of the Atlas Mountains, in an oasis city teeming with people and animals and sweltering outdoor markets. Kenji and Eiji had eleven hundred miles of desert to the south of them, and they would, in two months' time, walk every step of the way to the Niger border— some on roads, some on sand dunes, some through life-sustaining oases, with their date palms and natural springs and markets and people.

The view southward from Laghouat was of nothing but sand. As the men took their first glimpse of the great desert, they stood side by side and drank in the incredible, mysterious silence. Despite their nervousness, they didn't exchange a word for a few moments.

The Japanese travelers quickly learned how to tie the headdress of desert peoples, to keep themselves cool and protect their eyes from blowing sand. Because of the distances between the six oases—sometimes as far as two hundred miles—they used a rear cart, a sort of rickshaw that carries supplies rather than people. Among their supplies were three liters of water per person per day, half for cooking and half for drinking. To the cart, Kenji gradually added ten pounds of sand; he later published his observations of the granules that make up the Sahara in a Japanese geography journal.

Sometimes, on a good road surface, they would trade off pushing the cart. Other times, when they forced the cart through soft sand dunes, it took all they had to move it.

"Every ten steps we stop, rest," Kenji says.

But dunes made up only 20 percent of the desert; most of the walking was over hard ground, paved by the wind. Their desert days, dictated by the sun, went like this: Wake inside the tent at six a.m. Boil up water, mix in dry milk, eat a cookie. Pack up camp and leave. At ten a.m., stop for a break, eat an orange. At noon, when the sun was heating up the sand, spread peanut butter on French bread purchased in an oasis. Walk until sunset, make camp again.

Photos courtesy Kenji Yoshikawa

Food became an obsession for the travelers, who averaged about thirty miles each day. Because both men were adventurers in their twenties, their diet was not exciting.

"Ate bread and date and biscuit," Kenji says.

In oases, the trekkers would splurge for couscous in cafés. "We would think about it all day when walking," Kenji says. They would also purchase a new supply of fragrant, soft French bread that would last them for a few days. Toward the end of the bread's lifespan, however, it became so hard that it would cut their mouths ("Lots of pointy," Kenji says).

"I love [the bread] in oasis—so tasty—but four, five days later, almost stone," Kenji says. "Had to break by hammer."

Their French bread misadventures included the time when a parched Eiji shoved some dry bread in his mouth, tried to swallow, and then waved his arms at Kenji, eyes wide and pointing to his mouth. Sizing up the situation, Kenji grabbed a set of needlenose pliers from their tool kit. With them, he plucked a shard of bread from the back of Eiji's throat.

The vendors in the oasis markets sold no prepared foods. Spices were displayed in mounds and sold by weight; the young trekkers had no clue which to purchase. They chose what they knew—salt. Along with macaroni, it became their standard dinner.

"Every three days we have sardines with oil on top of macaroni," Kenji says. "That's heaven. The oil, so yummy to drink. Food is very poor, but our purpose was not food. Didn't care."

The men savored the sticky dates that grew at each oasis. They held them in their cheeks while walking, never getting thirsty even on the hottest days. They got so they could tell which dates—by their texture and stickiness—came from which oasis.

On the days between the date palms of the oases, there was no shade except for that provided by the Earth when evening fell.

"Day and night feel like two completely different worlds," Kenji says.

Because there was no promise of shade on most days, both men were surprised that they never felt hot. Nights were cold, as the heat of the day shimmered into space through clear skies, and they would eat their macaroni and salt and sometimes sardine oil while wearing down jackets and pants. The sky lit up with stars so bright Kenji thought he was in heaven. After they began walking, Kenji found a rhythm that spoke to his soul.

"Walking is really good for me," he says. "When walking you think about many things. Looking at landscape is fun, but more fun is looking inside [myself]. Thinking of college, my girlfriend, back to high school, back to primary school— tons of time to think. I think of how young my memory can go—three years old, four years old. Nothing to do but think. I'm super happy."

As he walked along, Kenji at times would realize he had a smile on his face. On a few of those occasions, he looked over and saw that Eiji was smiling, too.

"Biggest satisfaction is to see the dune, moon, typical desert. I really loved it. So happy every day. Every day, sun comes up, start walking, eat orange same time, macaroni and salt every night. I'd say, What's the difference between yesterday and today? No cloud, blue sky, sand, nothing else—completely same! What's the difference between yesterday and today? Nothing. That's really something. That made me very happy."

The consistent scenery removed all distractions from the travelers, and, as their bodies adapted to the rigors of the heat and the pushing and the daily miles, their minds drifted to more philosophical matters. Hearing the soothing, familiar chants of the Koran recited at the oases, Kenji thought of how natural it was that a major religion was born in the desert.

On some days, shoving the cart through the dunes, Kenji felt utterly insignificant, and he began to think that the nomads, who had only the few possessions they carried, were some of the freest people he had ever seen.

"Humans think they are the center of the Earth, because they can use tools, but in the desert, wind decides everything," Kenji says.

They would sit through sandstorms that would force them to keep their eyes and mouths closed, make movement impossible, and create so much static electricity that they were afraid to hand things to one another; six-inch sparks jumped the gap when they forgot. They also learned to set up their tent with its entrance toward the wind; when they pitched it with the zipper to the lee side, enough sand would gather there that they would have to dig their way out.

Kenji got in a groove broken pleasantly when he and Eiji would meet up with nomads who would offer them food.

"Felt like I was born in Sahara, walking every day. That's why I am here. I wanted to walk forever."

The travelers stopped two months after they started, when they reached the border of Niger. They had crossed the great desert, north to south, and Kenji felt a shift within him.

"Come back from desert, you are a different person," he says. "Something changes inside. You know that happiness is not material thing, food or water. It's very simple things."

■ ■ ■

One day, in the middle of their trip, the travelers lost the track of nomads and other oasis-goers. They kept wandering on across the sand, in the direction they believed was correct. On a break, sitting on a dune, Kenji looked back over the red

Photo courtesy Kenji Yoshikawa

sand and saw only their tracks, winding to the horizon. It was the most beautiful image he'd ever seen.

"It was so clean, no insects, so completely dry. I think this is maybe the best place in the world.

"Then I wondered, maybe snow makes the same beautiful thing, if the track goes away to horizon—maybe I should go to the Arctic. That day, I decided to go to the polar regions."

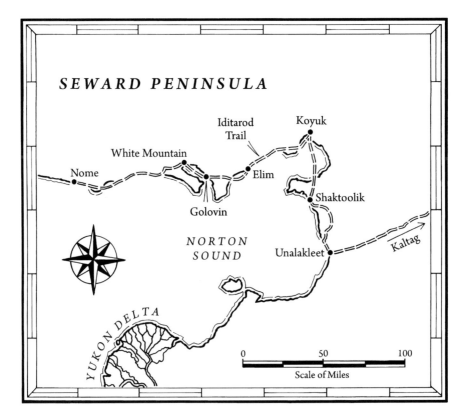

SEWARD PENINSULA

Koyuk

Iditarod
Trail

White Mountain

Nome

Elim

Golovin

Shaktoolik

NORTON
SOUND

Unalakleet

Kaltag

YUKON DELTA

0   50   100

Scale of Miles

Chapter Five

Wind Is the Eskimo's Friend

March in Shaktoolik. Snow is knifing sideways, stinging like shotgun pellets on your cheek. The locals say it has been storming for two weeks straight, and they seem fatigued, like people in Fairbanks who have pushed through the syrup of forty-below air for fifteen days, or Seattle residents grunging out their third straight week of rain. Can I get the darkest coffee you roast?

The weather station on the roof of the Shaktoolik school shows a wind speed of thirty-one miles per hour, which is enough to drive snow deep into your earholes if you wear only a baseball cap, which a few Native men do as they ride four wheelers over the cliffs of snow on Shaktoolik's only street.

An hour ago, it was a lovely clear day in the Blueberry Hills, just east of the village. Up there, Kenji, Tohru, and I were having one of our best travel days of this two-week journey. After seven days of moving through mostly treeless country, we left Unalakleet and ran into the Iditarod trail on a frozen slough outside of town.

The trail, marked with wooden stakes flagged with orange surveyor's tape, curved upward into the Blueberry Hills, leading into willows and scattered spruce trees. The trees, rare here on the coast that touches a cold northern sea, made us relax a bit, since in the worst winds we could hunker beneath them. Plus, we grew up with trees; there's a warmth and security that comes from being close to them. Since five days earlier in Emmonak, the scenery has been open white tundra, the shadows of our tracks the only relief. It's been like traveling behind high beams in dense fog.

In the Blueberry Hills, Kenji is satisfied enough with our progress that he pauses to take video clips of Tohru and me riding by on our snowmachines, with Norton Sound all white and blue in the background. Besboro Island floats out there like a whale on the sea ice, all lonely and beckoning someone to visit.

Tohru dismounts and kicks steps into a hill for a better view of Norton Sound, which is black with open water near the shoreline (and, because snowmachines don't float, the reason the winter trail cuts through the hills).

"Yeah, best day yet," Kenji says. "No wind!"

On what Iditarod mushers call "The Coast," the exposed chin beneath the nose of the Seward Peninsula, wind is the dominant feature, more noticeable to an outsider than the sea ice. The wind always blows, but in the Blueberry Hills we have a respite. And a visual clue that things are about to get uncomfortably normal again.

At the crest of a hill that allows a view of Shaktoolik, we stop the machines and look out toward the village. I have skied this part of the trail before. I know where the village should be, but we can't see it from the top of the hill. Instead, we see the bend of the coastline and the naked white flats surrounding Shaktoolik. Where the village sits, we see fuzzy whiteness, as if we are looking through binoculars left out in the rain.

"I think it's windy down there," I say.

Kenji nods.

Tohru Saito, with Besboro Island and Norton Sound in the background

"Might be end of good day," he says.

We drop down the hill, out of the trees, and onto the flats. In less than one minute, the day changes. A cold wind barracudas in from the northeast, nibbling through the cracks in our parkas. I hunch to the left, my head at the level of the handlebars, searching for the sweet spot where the windshield will stop the pain. With an ambient temperature of zero degrees, the wind won't kill us, but it will destroy some flesh on uncovered skin, first making it look sunburned, then peeling it off and revealing fresh pale skin underneath.

Kenji already has welts on the bridge of his nose and his upper cheeks, the places where his glasses touch his face. I feel bad for his wounds, since he gave me the wide-track machine with better flotation and an extended windshield. His windshield looks like it belongs on a toy snowmachine. But he has never mentioned his frostbite, and his fingertips never stray to that area of his face.

As we ride our snowmachines over frozen Beeson Slough, blank white and indistinguishable from land, we are entering a place with conditions foreign to anyone not from Shaktoolik.

Protected by our heavy parkas, boots, and goggles, we pass the rusted and bullet-holed truck that marks the entrance to Old Shaktoolik, a victim of climate

change before people thought change was unusual. As the wind rips through the weathered frame buildings—as it has for days before and days to come—Tohru points out a puppy huddling in the lee of a metal container that came into the country on a barge long ago. A staked-out dog team is nearby. Some dogs raise their heads and squint into the wind to watch us pass. They aren't having much fun today, and seem to have the fate of many unlucky village dogs. A shiver goes through me. *Poor pups.*

Old Shaktoolik is about two miles from the current village site, which is the latest in a long progression of places Shaktoolik has occupied. Nearby, a number of rich archaeological sites include Iyatayet, a place where archaeologists found flints and other artifacts from ancient peoples who lived near a creek on Cape Denbigh about six thousand years ago. A half-dozen more sites exist closer to present-day Shaktoolik, which for thirty years has occupied its space on the Tagoomenik River, now a short beluga drag from Norton Bay.

Until 1932, when the village council decided to move Shaktoolik in order to make receiving barge freight easier, the village was located at the mouth of the Shaktoolik River. After that, people lived in Old Shaktoolik, until flooding and wave erosion prompted the move one mile northwest, to a site whose advantage is not obvious in springtime.

Shaktoolik's location, in the teeth of a perpetual northeast gale, seems the oddest place for a village of any we have visited. Our main question, as the school anemometer squeaks through a steady workout, is "Why do people live here?"

Former Iditarod musher and writer Joe Runyan once pondered the same question. He wrote that Shaktoolik is "one of the most inconceivable communities in the world." In an Iditarod trail description, Runyan detailed an exchange with one of his Shaktoolik friends, Lynn Takuk, in which Runyan noticed that Takuk had gathered spruce firewood from a few dozen miles inland: "'Lynn, why don't you go to that big grove of spruce and get out of the wind? You could build a great cabin from those big logs.' I thought I was speaking and thinking cogently. Lynn and his boys chuckled politely. 'We like the wind. It brings us fish, and the animals like to be in the wind. The wind is the Eskimo's friend.'"

Sheltered in teacher Jake Doth's science classroom while Kenji gives a lecture, Tohru and I watch out the window as the road grader bites into snowdrifts on Shaktoolik's street. The wind starts filling the void immediately as the machine passes. Snow flows like a liquid over the fresh white cut of the blade.

As we watch what is to us a spectacle, Shaktoolik's mayor, Edgar Jackson, is a few buildings away. He is finishing a letter to Donny Olson, the local senator serving in Juneau.

"Currently, our snow-fence is 20 years old and rapidly deteriorating, creating a drastic hardship for our community with very high snowdrifts and in places close to our electrical power lines posing a threat to our children," Jackson wrote

in his request for funds to replace the fence, which stands in disjointed timbers east of town.

In town, the drifts eliminate the need for ladders if anyone needs to reach a roof, and a gymnast could vault to the power lines from snowbanks. In his request to build a new thirty-two-hundred-foot snow fence to deflect more of the snow before it reaches the village, Mayor Jackson encloses a quote from Spenard Builders Supply in Anchorage: four hundred treated twenty-foot six-by-sixes and eighty-six hundred treated sixteen-foot two-by-fours, barged from Seattle straight to Shaktoolik. The invoice totals $199,419.48.

Kenji speaks to two classes of students in the Shaktoolik School, giving the lecture on permafrost he modifies a bit for each group of kids. The Shaktoolik high schoolers are mostly Native, with a few white students, likely related to teachers. As in many villages, few people live here who were not born here.

Kenji wears black canvas work pants and a gray work shirt, along with a black Under Armour skullcap. Beneath the hat, he is a skinhead by choice rather than heredity; he shaved for a homemade video in which he appears as "Tunnel Man," a superhero who emerges from a permafrost tunnel, dusts himself off, and is soon dog-mushing, snowmachining, and shooting arrows into the air while straddling a pile of snow.

Without his Tunnel Man costume, Kenji's shaved head and stocky build make him look like someone you'd go out of your way not to annoy. So far on this trip, he's showed the abilities and toughness you would expect of a world traveler who has powered across some of its most difficult surfaces on foot.

His fingers are tough as raven's feet. Before falling asleep on the floor of school classrooms, he repairs his cracked fingernails with Super Glue. When he melts plastic tubing with a torch to prepare his frost tubes, he quenches the molten plastic with his fingertips. His feet seem to have the same indifference; a few nights ago he burst outside the Unalakleet school gym in bare feet, stepping on metal grating. It was ten below. He stood there and took a photo of the orange moon over Norton Sound, then walked back inside the gym. With no complaints, he's worn thin rubber boots since we started, even on the minus-eighteen morning in St. Michael. His warmer boots were part of the shipment that didn't arrive in Emmonak (and a day ago didn't arrive in Unalakleet, either). It seems obvious that this person has weathered a lot of storms, along with insects, leeches, bad food, dangerous people, and complicated logistics. He doesn't make a big deal out of anything.

■   ■   ■

Finishing his lecture, Kenji gives a nod to Tohru, standing with me near the back of the classroom. It's time to drill.

"He's got to be kidding, right?" I ask Tohru. "It's still a hurricane out there."

"Nope," Tohru says with a pained smile. "Not kidding."

Kenji's uniqueness is starting to sink in now. Most scientists would relax in the diesel-fired warmth of a village school for a few hours when the ambient temperature was zero and the wind was blowing thirty miles per hour. Tweak some equipment. Read a book maybe. Not Kenji. We're going out.

As we get ready, I have flashbacks. Eight years ago to the day, I waited out a similar storm, in a teacher's house here in Shaktoolik. Three of my friends were skiing from Anchorage to Nome, and I flew into Shaktoolik to join them for the glory stretch. As we approached Shaktoolik from Unalakleet in the twin-engine plane, the pilot said, "Your friends must be pretty soft if they're thinking about not going because of the wind."

Then he almost flipped the plane while landing in a crosswind on the Shaktoolik strip. He looked over at me with wide eyes when the plane rolled to a halt, gusts rocking it as if polar bears were jumping on the wings. "Oh, now I see why they aren't moving."

I strapped my skis to a guy's wooden sled behind his sno-go, and he knew to take me to the teacher's house before I asked him. There, my friends and I waited three days for the wind to mellow somewhat.

I remember the days of waiting, watching *Uncle Buck* and a dozen other movies as we killed time, and wearing goggles on trips to the Shaktoolik Native Store for frozen pizzas. Those hikes to the store seemed as hazardous as ventures outside the tent during a storm at Denali's High Camp. After three days, when we could make out the faint outline of the wooden tripod marking the way to Koyuk, we snuck out on cold snow and had a squeaky ski to a cabin fourteen miles out, each of us saying a silent prayer that the wind would stay away. We felt as if we were tiptoeing out on a beach after the tsunami had passed. But snowmachine travel is different from skiing—heavy parkas snuff the wind's bite, and with a machine you can run away from danger (you can skip across open water, for example, which is hard to do on skis without a boat pulling you).

I follow Kenji and Tohru to the classroom in which we've left our heavy clothes. If it were up to me, I'd stay inside eating ramen and looking at the pictures of village elders on the walls. But it's not up to me. Kenji's trip schedule—and his personality—won't wait. We pull on our big boots, our snowmachine coveralls, our parkas, our hats, face masks, and big mittens. Before walking outside, Kenji pulls up his parka hood, lined with polar bear fur, and shoves open the metal door of the school.

Stepping outside is like stepping into a Lilliputian shooting range where the riflemen are letting loose with a barrage of tiny white bullets. The wind forces you to turn away, but snowmachine coveralls and goggles and parkas snuff it, making traveling somewhat plausible, as long as your machine doesn't strand you out on the tundra.

As we wait for teacher Jake Doth, a tall, confident guy in his early thirties who's been in Shaktoolik for several years, Kenji sits on his snowmachine with his back to the wind. He yanks forward the hood of his parka. He then kicks his feet up on the handlebars of his machine and strikes an uncharacteristic relaxed pose. If the wind wasn't shrieking and he wasn't wearing thirty pounds of clothing in the middle of an Eskimo village, he could be on a beach in Australia.

Jake returns, and we ride over the forehead-high ridges of snow on Shaktoolik's street, headed for the tundra near Old Shaktoolik. Kenji, seeing everything, had on the ride in eyed the spot as a good place for a permafrost observatory.

Riding over the street is comical—you climb a small mountain of rock-hard snow and then drop off the backside, traveling twenty feet to progress ten feet down

the street. And the canyons are abrupt; a white cliff in the middle of the street forces me to yank my machine into reverse at its edge before I plunge over the top.

Tohru passes me after I get cliffed out. I can't hear him because of the howling wind, but his spasmodic head bobs suggest he is laughing at me and my machine, its skis suspended in midair as I back off the ledge. *Beep, beep, beep.*

We push through the narrow street, past frame buildings painted pastel colors and ravaged by the wind, and are back on the tundra, which is not drifted as badly as the village. Kenji motors to what seems to be a random spot of low vegetation, and there he stops. Jake pulls next to him, and Tohru and I follow on our machines.

Satisfied that he can remember the place so he can help maintain the station and use it in classroom exercises, Jake waves and motors off, the wind swallowing the noise of his machine.

There, in the Shaktoolik-strength wind, the practiced process of drilling a permafrost observatory begins. This is where Tohru shines, anticipating Kenji's every move and, when problems arise, offering his opinions, usually in Japanese. Working with his back to the wind, Tohru removes threaded drill shafts from a canvas rifle case while Kenji starts up a Honda generator and then assembles and plugs in his handheld drill, about as large as a two-year-old boy but twice as heavy.

Tohru, the rare trail partner who smiles even in the worst of times, needs to practice his good nature on this day. The top pocket of his insulated flannel shirt is unbuttoned; it flaps in the wind like a ptarmigan's wing as Tohru and Kenji try to separate two frozen sections of drill shaft. Tohru yanks on the lower portion of the extension while Kenji strikes the upper part with a hammer. When the frozen pieces come apart, Tohru rocks back like he's taken a punch. The process of drilling a four-meter hole is a forty-minute job on a warm sunny day. Today, it will take hours.

I turn my back to the wind and see an old fish rack in the distance. On it is a blue tarp, in tatters, its tendrils dancing in the breeze like kelp flowing in a rip tide. It's loud out here, with the wind giving voice to the snapping fragments of tarp, and it makes me think of something—it is nuts to be working in this wind. But there is Kenji, leaning into that drill, forcing it into the icy soil with all the muscles in his lower back. And he is here by choice. No boss back at the university has ordered him to be in Shaktoolik today. Kenji is the boss.

Here, it again becomes apparent that Kenji is creating his own reality. Many of his childhood friends are jamming themselves into Tokyo train cars twice a day, and many of them would probably describe themselves as happy. But their existence is more comfort-oriented, less risky, and probably less rewarding than that of the man who is shoving a drill into the ground in this big blow.

The drill slowly penetrates gray dirt flecked with ice crystals, gaining an inch every ten seconds or so. Tohru stands by, occasionally using his mittens to brush away frozen soil, which leaps into the air and travels a few hundred feet before gravity pulls it back to Earth.

After a few hours, a few bad words absorbed by the wind, a few wind-adjusted spurts of WD-40, and lots of metal hammer tapping, Kenji has a twelve-foot hole. Into the hole, he and Tohru slip a plastic pipe, and into that snake a string of cable with thermometers. Kenji connects the thermistor cables to a few palm-size computer dataloggers that will record temperatures for a long time. Lacking the four-inch PVC pipe that he prefers, Kenji covers the dataloggers and wire with another provocative metal coffee can. Then we clean up.

The wind has blown on, never wavering in energy. It is like a living creature, relentless and uncaring, forcing equatorial creatures like me to crave shelter. I day-dream about sitting at a plastic classroom desk with a microwaved cheeseburger.

With everything buttoned up, we start our machines, which amaze us by firing up right away, and we creep, single file, back toward Shaktoolik. Tohru leads. Kenji is in the rear.

As I move through Old Shaktoolik, a sheet of plywood flies toward my windshield. I duck, and what I thought was plywood but is in fact a heavy-duty tarp blasts by on its way to Russia. I squint ahead and see that the lid has popped off the ActionPacker wedged behind Tohru's seat. He is unaware of this development, and continues on. Hammers, dataloggers, thermistor cables, and other assorted items leap out of the ActionPacker as Tohru's machine bumps over the drifts, a failed bungee cord whipping behind. I yell, not expecting him to hear me for the layers of cotton and nylon around his ears, the hum of his machine, and the blasting of the wind. He doesn't slow his machine. The erup-tion of equipment continues.

I stop, dismount, and chase some of the gear in my heavy boots. The hammer stays where it fell, but everything else is on the move. I field a tumbleweeding bag of thermistor cables, but give up on smaller stuff that rolls past. I watch Tohru as he continues back to town, unaware. Kenji catches up with me and helps pick things up.

In a few minutes, Tohru shows up on foot. I hand him the ActionPacker lid and we all gather as much as we are able. Some things, like the tarp, are headed overseas. Maybe a Kamchatkan reindeer herder will use it to patch his roof.

Such is the price of doing business in a brewing ground blizzard. And, though we lost a few things in the wind, Tohru has gained a nickname, which cracks us up later in the evening, when we can hear each other speak. He is now Yard Sale Saito.

We idle the machines back to Shaktoolik, stopping at the Native store to gas up our machines for the next day. A teenage boy goes outside to start the pump for us, and we watch snow crystals flow into the gas tanks as if a vacuum is pulling them in. Back in the store, as Tohru laughs at an icicle bridging from my mous-tache to my beard, Kenji pays the boy several hundred dollars for the gas.

Returning to the shelter of the school, we cook up burritos in the microwave and Kenji and Tohru break out some village-store Neapolitan ice cream (Tohru calls it "Napoleon") that probably began life in a factory in Pennsylvania and made it to the Shaktoolik Native store by truck, train, plane, and snowmachine or four-wheeler. We eat a few bowls to help me celebrate my forty-fifth birthday, just a few weeks before Kenji's forty-fifth.

As we clean up the school kitchen and get ready to roll out our sleeping mats, Kenji announces that he's going back outside into the wind, a thought as appeal-ing as grabbing a book and slipping into a tub of ice water.

"Need to download the dataloggers," he says.

"Do you want me to go with you?" Tohru asks, gallantly.

"No, I'll be back in little while," Kenji says.

I say nothing. My silence is conspicuous, and I feel like a weenie, but I've had enough of that wind. And, hey, it's my birthday.

After a few minutes of pulling on coveralls and parka, Kenji shoves open the door of the school. Snow blasts inside and clings to the carpet; the wind hasn't let up—the anemometer clinging to the roof has read between twenty-five and forty mph for the past six hours.

Kenji disappears into the blowing snow and throws a heavy leg over his machine. I pull the door shut behind him. It's like sealing the entrance to a space ship, trapping the life-giving warmth inside. I feel a twinge of guilt, but my shame disappears before the snow melts on the carpet.

Amid the moan of wind through power lines, we hear the faint whine of a snowmachine firing to life. The engine wavers, and then fades away. The blowing snow swallows Kenji's taillight. He merges with the storm, and then disappears.

■ ■ ■

Might the cold, unpeopled Arctic be as barren and beautiful as the Sahara? Kenji, remembering those tracks in the dunes, had to find out. Knowing nothing about the cold, or the world north of Hokkaido, he would attempt a walk in the Arctic, in search of the magnetic North Pole. Less confident people, a group that includes almost seven billion, do not entertain such dreams. But how else do you prepare for Mars?

Because the Earth is a giant ball hosting a smaller, rotating, moon-size ball of nickel and iron at its core, its magnetism is not the same now as it was five minutes ago. Though these forces are too subtle to detect without expensive instruments, they affect the planet's magnetic poles. The magnetic North Pole—the place to where a compass needle points—is always on the move, and is never quite the same from year to year.

The magnetic pole migrates in fits and starts, usually to the northwest; it has wandered about the north for thousands of years. In 1986, it was about 240 miles northwest of the village of Resolute Bay, on Cornwallis Island in Canada's High Arctic.

After returning to southern Japan from the Sahara, Kenji noticed an airport symbol near the words Resolute Bay on his Michelin world map. He stuck a pin there. Dream kindled, all he needed was a ticket north.

All the sweat and energy and mental power he once poured into boxing, Kenji now invested in making money.

He remembers those days and sultry Okinawa nights as a blur—tutoring kids in the afternoon, spending his nights at the front desk of the hotel, then working a few hours smoothing asphalt under floodlights at a road construction job. His days were the classes and tests and labs of a full-time college student.

"Very little sleeping," he says. "Almost no."

He worked so hard because he knew an arctic trip would be much more expensive than the Sahara. He could live on petrified bread and dates in the desert, easily spending a dollar each day or less, but the cold of the Arctic required more funds, starting with the ticket from Okinawa to Tokyo to Los Angeles to Edmonton to Resolute Bay.

He consulted Kohshiro Kizaki, the University of the Ryukyus professor who had weathered antarctic expeditions and the high country of the Himalayas. He asked Kizaki how to keep his flesh from freezing in temperatures he couldn't yet imagine. The coldest air Kenji had ever felt was in the high twenties Fahrenheit in Tokyo.

"Cold is biggest unknown factor at that time," he says.

In an attempt to remedy that, he asked a friend who owned a store if he would mind if Kenji hung out in his walk-in freezer, the air of which lingered in the midteens. Thinking Kenji was crazy but won over by his enthusiasm, his friend told him to go ahead, live in the freezer. Kenji spent afternoons in the deep-freeze, reading books, and exercising when he got chilled. He slept in the freezer just once, fearing there wouldn't be enough fresh air to last the night.

While the walk-in freezer was probably the closest he could get to Resolute Bay while living on Okinawa, he later learned it was a poor substitute for the high Arctic.

"No wind," he says.

Kenji had camped in snow in the mountains of northern Honshu. It was a damp, maritime variety of snow. He had also shivered himself slim on more than one camping trip with the Boy Scouts. But he was still an utter novice, and he knew it.

He fashioned a sled after reading history books of northern explorers. It consisted of a platform that rode above the snow on two skis. He purchased three sleeping bags, stuffed with goose down, from an American base exchange. In his dorm room one evening, he took his knife and sliced open each compartment of two of the sleeping bags. He removed all the feathers from two bags and piled them on his bed. Then he strategically sliced the third bag and, through the slits, stuffed the feathers from the other two bags. The mummy bag was then super-puffed, as hard as a cocoon. He slithered in as far as he could, but stopped before the bag enveloped his broad shoulders.

"Couldn't get in," he says. "It was very poor idea."

Undeterred, Kenji continued to consult with Kizaki, experiment with gear, and work like a dairy farmer. The pile of yen notes under his sleeping mat grew, and in a few months he had earned enough for the ticket to Resolute Bay.

In late February, after a quick visit with his concerned and bemused parents in Tokyo, he was on his way to arctic Canada.

■ ■ ■

If you were to stand at the magnetic North Pole, or venture within a few hundred miles of it, the needle of your compass would dip straight downward; you'd have to tilt it to float the needle, and you wouldn't think of it as much of a tool. Kenji knew this, and in those days before GPS, he would use an automatic direction finder antenna, a device that uses radio signals broadcast from different areas to triangulate a person's location. This device, he thought, would help him find his way back to the village of Resolute Bay after he'd reached the magnetic pole and turned around.

The magnetic North Pole has been a moving target of adventurers for centuries. In 1600, Sir William Gilbert, a doctor for Queen Elizabeth I, was the first to suggest Earth behaved like a giant magnet. In 1829, another Brit, Sir John Ross, commanded an expedition to find the Northwest Passage from the Atlantic to the Pacific. He didn't slip through the passage, as ice trapped his ship in Canada's Arctic for four years. Before the ships were able to retreat to England, Ross's nephew, James Ross, discovered the magnetic North Pole on another mission. When Norwegian Roald Amundsen found the same point during the first successful trip through the Northwest Passage seventy years later, in 1904, magnetic north had staggered thirty miles north of where Ross found it.

At the time Kenji attempted to reach the magnetic pole, no one to his knowledge had pulled off the feat by foot (or ski). And, being that it was less than three hundred miles from Resolute Bay, Kenji viewed the magnetic pole as a reachable goal. The mission would etch another landscape into his memory.

Kenji was soon on a jet, his bags packed with food from an Edmonton supermarket. He flew north above the spruce and birch of the boreal forest and beads of small, frozen lakes. His forehead pasted to the window, he watched as the trees below petered out to spindly black spruce. He flew over Great Slave Lake, the deepest lake in North America at minus two thousand feet, and continued north-ward, passing over the imaginary line of the Arctic Circle. By then, trees were a memory, as was everything else familiar. He felt an excitement that bordered on terror, and he smiled to himself—he was living the best way he knew.

After a few more hours, the small plane bounced down on a gravel runway, and Kenji looked out the window to see what was his first village of northern Native people.

Resolute Bay is one of the coldest towns in the world, with an average yearly temperature of just 2.5 degrees Fahrenheit (Fairbanks's average is about twenty-eight degrees, Denver's fifty, New Orleans's a perfect sixty-eight), and it is an arti-ficial town to some extent. Named after a British Royal Navy ship, Resolute Bay is one of three far north outposts that were sites of Inuit relocation from northern Quebec in the 1950s, with the goal of having people farther north during the cold war. Canadian officials believed the presence of the Inuit would discourage Greenland, the United States, and Denmark from making claims on Cornwallis Island, upon which sits the site of Resolute Bay, and Ellesmere Island, the site of two other experimental villages.

The forced move to Resolute Bay in 1953 was a rough one, as the Inuit of the northern Quebec Barrenlands were not familiar with the extreme far north landscape, which was flat and windy and thin in caribou and musk oxen and other creatures needed for life. It was also painful for other reasons, as Melanie McGrath wrote in her book, *The Long Exile: A Tale of Inuit Betrayal and Survival in the High Arctic.*

> By the mid-sixties almost every Inuit family in Resolute Bay had been affected by alcoholism. Things got so bad at the Inuit settlement that in some homes there was nothing to eat for days except the chewing gum the airmen handed out to the chil-dren to keep them quiet while they had sex with their mothers. A whole generation of Inuit children were left to bring up themselves while their fathers and mothers descended into squalor and depression. . . . In the nine years from 1953 to 1962, fifty Inuit girls and boys were born in Resolute Bay. Thirty years later, nearly a third of them were already dead.

Into this place, called Qausuittuq ("place with no dawn") in the Native Inuk-titut, at two a.m. on a February morning, dropped Kenji. As the pilot sliced the wings into a ripping headwind, the plane touched down. Kenji and a few other passengers filed off the plane, down a protected walkway, and into the airport.

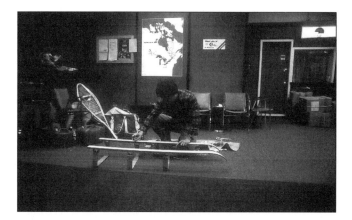

Kenji assembling gear in the Resolute Bay airport. Photo courtesy Kenji Yoshikawa.

A door slid open, allowing cold air to penetrate the one-room terminal. A baggage handler shoved in Kenji's bag and the taped-up bundle of his sled parts. In the early morning hours, fewer than a dozen people were in the airport. The only noises were a few muffled coughs, the soft conversation of people picking up their relatives, and the hum of fluorescent lights.

Here was one of those stark, lonely moments that come in the life of an adventurer—half a world away from home, groggy and unsure in a dark little air terminal that smelled of cigarette smoke. He felt the eyes of others upon him.

As Kenji assembled his sled, preparing to embark on his adventure from the terminal, a Native man dressed in a parka approached him.

"Do you speak English?" the man asked.

"Yes," Kenji said.

"Where are you going?"

Kenji told him of his journey, and the man nodded thoughtfully.

"It's blowing pretty good out there," he said. "Cold too, about minus thirty-five. You might want to be careful if you go out."

Kenji bowed to the man, shook his hand, and the man walked off. Kenji finished assembling his sled, and napped until daylight. He was ready to move. He dressed in his cold-weather gear, and took a few deep breaths before starting out.

He pulled his sled out the door and into a different atmosphere. The wind knifed in from the infinite cold pool near the pole, biting his nose and eyes and the skin of his wrists that his coat didn't cover. He pulled at his clothing to stop the bee stings, and pushed forward against the wind, in a direction he thought would lead him out of town. He bumped into something with his sled, then looked down and saw his plastic camera case had shattered in the cold. That never happened in the walk-in cooler.

Kenji trudged on into the wind and felt a sharp pain at the tip of his nose that waned as quickly as it appeared. He touched his nose with his mitten and felt nothing. He felt a flash of panic and stopped, his sled skidding behind him.

In this, his first taste of the Arctic, Kenji was experiencing something he'd never dreamed of. The wind, along with a temperature of minus thirty degrees, made standing outside unbearable. The heat of his movement would help, but how would a person pitch a tent in this? And, looking around, Kenji saw no other people outside. It reminded him of when the desert nomads would stop moving when the wind picked up, wrap their faces in their headdresses, and hunker down during a sandstorm.

He stopped. He turned around. After moving less than a quarter mile, he headed back to the dim shelter of the air terminal. He dragged his sled back inside, shaking his head. He peeled off his hat and felt his face. The longer he lingered in the heated building, the more intense the fire on his nose and cheeks. After just a few minutes of exposure, the far north had left its mark.

"Already I am frostbite, first day," Kenji says.

The next morning, Kenji met a meteorologist, who later introduced him to some of the local Inuit. A Native man suggested that Kenji stay in town for a few days, and used snow blocks to construct an igloo with Kenji's help, at the edge of the village. Kenji stayed in the igloo, took his meals with the family, and became friends with one of the man's sons, who was about twelve years old. The family gave him tips on how to survive the cold (and when to avoid moving), and he observed for the first time a northern subsistence lifestyle.

"It was a very strong impression," he says.

As he adapted to the high arctic spring, Kenji made plans for his trek to the northwest, to the blank spot on the sea ice that was the magnetic North Pole.

Then he experienced some cold friction, because of an item he had brought with him. Knowing he would be traveling North America after attempting the magnetic pole, Kenji carried with him a set of *nunchaku*, also known as "nunchucks." Kenji was a big fan of Bruce Lee, who was so adept at using the two shafts of wood connected by a chain that he could beat expert table-tennis players using nunchucks as a paddle.

Kenji had developed a talent for nunchucks in Okinawa as part of his boxing regimen. He figured he could perform with them on the streets of big cities to maybe earn some cash. As his Inuit little buddy was interested in karate, Kenji performed with the nunchucks in the family home. The boy insisted that Kenji come to his school and twirl the nunchucks at an assembly.

Kenji wowed the kids of the school, but he also caught the attention of a Resolute Bay policeman who saw a powerful young man twirling a weapon that, unknown to Kenji, was illegal for him to carry into Canada. Though he didn't dream of it at the time, that appearance at a student assembly would snuff out his trip.

"You need a gun for your trip," Kenji's Inuit friend told him one afternoon while standing outside Kenji's igloo. "Those white bears don't eat tundra. Only meat. And you're it, out there moving slow with no protection."

Kenji didn't have a shotgun, but he had thought about it before and knew he would need a permit to carry one. His Inuit friends had a gun to loan him. With one month's food packed on his sled and his navigation equipment on top where he could easily reach it, Kenji was ready to begin his quest for magnetic north. To sew up the one remaining detail, he walked over to the police station to get his permit to carry the shotgun.

Walking up to the counter, Kenji recognized the policeman from the crowd at the assembly where he had performed with the nunchucks. As one of the few adults at Kenji's performance, Kenji had noticed him, and that the man had frowned throughout the assembly. The policeman was afraid of this young foreigner who so skillfully twirled the nunchucks. He saw Kenji as a threat.

"You brought a weapon into Canada," the policeman said. "I will let you keep that in your possession, because you haven't caused any trouble yet. But I will not give you the permit for the gun."

Kenji pleaded his case politely, speaking of polar bears and danger and his dream, but the policeman stood there, arms folded, listening impassively.

"No permit. I am sorry."

Kenji slunk out of the office, his mind reeling.

Maybe I should go anyway. Maybe I don't need a gun.

He walked back to the home of the Inuit family, and told them of his plight. The father picked up the phone, speaking to his friends about the unfairness of the situation. Kenji soon had several villagers lobbying for him, and felt good about his chances.

But the policeman wouldn't budge. Kenji got no permit. With time for his trip running out, and after hearing several stories about polar bears pursuing people, Kenji abandoned his plan to reach the magnetic pole.

At that moment, Kenji could have moped and made plans to return to Okinawa. But instead of flying out of Resolute Bay, he stayed for a month. He had

Bottom: Resolute Bay
Photos courtesy Kenji Yoshikawa

plenty of food that he had bought in Edmonton, and he wanted to eat it all up before leaving. Instead of heading for the pole, he embarked on a shorter trip, staying on the outskirts of the village but still getting out on his own.

The dunes of snow he saw outside Resolute Bay reminded him of the Sahara, as did the utter silence during the few moments when the wind wasn't blowing. He became interested in the landforms under that snow, and documented them all in a notebook. The work became part of his bachelor's thesis at college, as he examined the geomorphology of shapes on the island.

Satisfied he had accomplished something, Kenji pulled his sled—which had the fatal flaw of tipping when it ran over the slightest bit of sastrugi drift—back to Resolute Bay.

After a month in the high Arctic, he flew to Yellowknife, where the road system began. As the plane lifted off from the snow-covered flats, Kenji reflected on his time north of the Arctic Circle.

"In general, my feeling is [that I was a] loser, I can't make it," he says. "But maybe a little more strong feeling is that Arctic is terribly difficult. You need lots of knowledge, and you need skills, I thought later it turned into a very good trip for all I learned there."

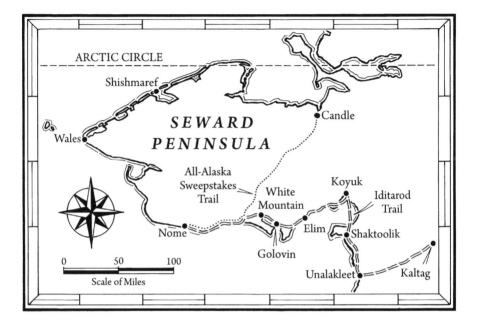

ARCTIC CIRCLE

Shishmaref

Wales

SEWARD
PENINSULA

Candle

All-Alaska
Sweepstakes
Trail

White
Mountain

Koyuk

Iditarod
Trail

Elim

Shaktoolik

Nome

Golovin

Unalakleet

Kaltag

0   50   100

Scale of Miles

Chapter Six

Dare to Fail

Nome. Stampede City. Beaches with gold in the sand. The breezy hub of the Seward Peninsula. Where Alaska rubs noses with Russia.

This gold rush outpost, born in 1899, looks like it needs a nap. Many of the buildings on Front Street had their last coat of paint applied in the 1970s, when the Iditarod was gaining steam. Nome of the 2000s is waiting for another boom.

This morning, though, there's a sense of anticipation. City workers have mined snow from the outskirts of town and, using dump trucks, deposited it on Front Street. The knuckled sprucewood arch used to mark the finish of the Iditarod, which for most of the year is standing parallel to the sidewalk in front of a Nome city government building, is standing in the middle of Front Street. Someone has stretched a yellow race banner beneath its spans.

In a few hours, at ten a.m., for the first time since 1983 and the second time since 1917, the All Alaska Sweepstakes dogsled race will start in Nome. The Sweepstakes, celebrating its hundredth anniversary, features a 408-mile out-and-back course, no dog drops (if a pup gets tired or hurt or dies, you carry it on your sled), winner takes $100,000. Second place gets no money. Some big names in the mushing world are here to try for that prize, which—for an event that will take the winner two days—is more than the combined purses of the Iditarod and Yukon Quest.

We are up early and have packed our bags and loaded them on the snowmachines. Kenji wants to make it to Brevig Mission tonight, after a drilling stop in Teller. Teller is sixty miles away, Brevig Mission six more.

I would love to watch the start of the All Alaska Sweepstakes, because I probably won't be here for the next one, if they stage a 125th-anniversary race in 2033. The race goes from Nome to Candle and back, with Nome being the only checkpoint that is still a town, unlike Boston, Haven, First Chance, Timber, and Topkok. So it has that Alaska ghost-town appeal, plus I'm curious as to whether Lance Mackey can win the race after winning both the Yukon Quest and the Iditarod, an absurd feat because both races are more than a thousand miles long, they're less than one month apart, and Mackey uses many of the same dogs to run both races. That's like asking your dogs to pull you from Maine to Colorado, with the temperature dipping to minus forty in Ohio and the winds ripping through Kansas at seventy miles per hour.

Here in Nome, with Jeff King, Mitch Seavey, and other top mushers eyeballing their flown-in dogs and mentally assembling their teams, drama is building. But we won't see it. Kenji wants us to be gone an hour before the race starts. He's already scouted a way out of town that doesn't use Front Street, where the mushers will be; we will be driving northwest, on a snow-covered road toward Teller, as the mushers are heading southwest, toward Cape Nome.

All packed, Tohru and I sneak out to the Polar Café for a quick breakfast and a break from food we've been microwaving in teachers' lounges at all the schools. As soon as we walk in the door of the restaurant, butted up against Nome's frozen seawall, we recognize two people seated at the one occupied table: Lance Mackey and his wife, Tonya.

I have met Lance before, when I interviewed him for an *Alaska* magazine feature after the first time he won both the Quest and the Iditarod. When I met him for the first time at Hilltop Café, famous for its FatMan pie, he was open and forthright. That surprised me, after interviewing other mushers, like Jeff King, who would reveal little during an interview and then break out secrets during the race—like his use of a European skijor harness system that allowed his dogs to pull from their shoulders rather than the base of their tails.

Lance became easy to root for as he started doing what others thought was impossible—winning both major distance mushing races in the same year and, an even more impressive feat, recovering from cancer and becoming a family man when the odds were against him in both.

The widest street in Nome is a special place for Lance. When he was eight, his dad, Dick Mackey, in the Iditarod's only sprint finish, charged down Front Street twenty yards from where Lance sits now. In black-and-white photos of the 1978 event, Dick's nostrils are flaring beneath his wild eyes, whip in hand, as he coaxes his dogs to run down the chute along with Rick Swenson's. Officials declared Dick the winner by one second, as the nose of his lead dog crossed the finish first.

Lance's half-brother, Rick Mackey, also passed over Front Street a winner, in 1983. Wanting to repeat the victory he had seen his role models accomplish, Lance camped out near Iditarod headquarters in Wasilla for one month during the summer of 2007. He wanted the right to choose the number thirteen, which both his father and his brother were wearing when they won their only Iditarods, each on his sixth attempt. Lance was first to sign up, and 2007 was Lance's first Iditarod win, also on his sixth attempt, wearing lucky number thirteen.

When I spoke with Lance a few years ago, he described his comeback from a tumor in his neck that made him black out in pain; his starting up of a new life with his childhood sweetheart, her children, and no money, the clan camping on a beach on the Kenai Peninsula where he was thankful not to be evicted; his winning of the two biggest dog races in the world two years in a row; and the fact that he knows it's no small thing to be among the living.

"I believe I'm really lucky to be here," Lance said. "It sounds corny, but I look forward to every single day."

After Tohru and I finish eating, we see that Lance, Tonya, and a few of their dog handlers are rising from their seats. I approach their table, and Lance wears the half smile of someone who has experience receiving fans. I shake his hand and ask to take his photo. I'm nervous as Lance and Tonya hug for the camera. He is, in my world, a celebrity.

"Good luck in the race," I say.

"Yeah, you guys have a great day, too," Lance says while zipping his jacket. "Looks like a nice one out there."

During the next two days, Lance will not win the All Alaska Sweepstakes (Mitch Seavey is first, with Jeff King second and Lance third), and he will face one of the most stressful events of his mushing career. Less than twenty-two miles from the finish, as he is nearing Nome, a snowmachiner using the same trail will gain on him, closing like he somehow can't see Lance standing on his sled.

"I was flashing them like mad with my headlamp," Lance told an *Anchorage Daily News* reporter. "I was shining my headlamp right in his face, but they kept on coming at me. I jumped aside, and by 30 feet farther up the trail, there was a snowmachine sitting on the middle of my sled.

"Three or four dogs were sucked underneath, and Zorro was trapped in the sled bag," he continued. "We had to physically remove [the snowmachine] from the sled."

His dog Zorro, who had fathered more dogs than any other in his yard, sustained injuries that forced Lance to fly the dog to Seattle for treatment. Zorro later recovered, but would never race again. Regardless, Lance won the Iditarod a third straight time the next year (after sitting out the Yukon Quest).

As Lance leaves the Polar Café for his upcoming adventure, I think of the similarities between him and the man we're traveling with.

Kenji is somewhat like Lance: neither waits for the world to come to him. Nor do they dwell on the fear of what might happen when their plans begin unraveling. They have improvised many times before, and are at their best when doing so.

Lance's handlers at home didn't keep his Iditarod dogs in good shape after he ran the Yukon Quest in 2007, so he harnessed up an almost identical team of hardheaded mile-eaters for the Iditarod. He called it "a blessing in disguise" when the Iditarod trail was unusually cold and unbroken along a few remote stretches, which favored his Quest dogs over the sleeker dogs in other teams. In Kenji's latest example, he has progressed throughout this trip without two-thirds of the equipment he was planning to bring (and is still stuck in Anchorage). He hasn't complained out loud once.

Both have mastered an established system: Lance dominates races that pay money and are scheduled years in advance; Kenji has the skills to convince individuals or science foundations to fund or otherwise help with his adventures. Both men live the credo of Norman Vaughan, the Alaska musher and adventurer who died four days after his one hundredth birthday in 2005: "Dream big, and dare to fail."

■ ■ ■

His food supply exhausted in Resolute Bay, and with nothing left to prove there after his failed attempt on the magnetic pole, Kenji flew to Yellowknife, a city on Great Slave Lake that is home to fifteen thousand people. More important to him,

Yellowknife has a road connection to the rest of North America. He wanted to see more of the continent before he flew to Los Angeles, where he would sniff out an inexpensive flight to Rio. In South America, at roughly the spot a bit would poke through if one were to drill straight down from Tokyo, Kenji would attempt another feat no adventurer had attempted.

First, though, he needed to get to Los Angeles. Yellowknife is the northern terminus of Canada's Greyhound bus line. Kenji planned to explore the continent with that conveyance, at least as far south as Los Angeles.

The twenty-three-year-old rode the bus to Edmonton. In the big (by northern Canada's standards) city he looked at the rate for buses south and was disappointed that the buses would cost more than one dollar for every fifty kilometers they would carry him, his personal benchmark for motor-coach travel.

He thought it might be cheaper to buy a motorcycle. In the *Edmonton Sun* newspaper, he found an ad for a Yamaha 400 that was less expensive than a bus ticket to Calgary.

He climbed on the bike and headed through Banff National Park, where his clutch slipped on a steep hill. It was the first of many problems with his discount ride.

"Lots of break," he says. "Which was really good for learning stuff."

He rattled through the Rockies and over to the West Coast of the United States. In the States for the first time, he marveled at the beauty of his campsite on the Oregon coast, the rugged cliffs meeting the roaring ocean. He motored through California, traveling within one hundred miles of the woman he would marry a few decades later.

He continued down to Los Angeles and sleuthed out the cheapest ticket to Rio de Janeiro for $300. Soon, he was boarding a plane with a tattered backpack and a pair of flip-flops.

As he followed a jetstream of warm air to another continent, he sipped a Coke with ice from a plastic cup, closed his eyes, and went over his plan.

He wanted to traverse the Amazon, the world's largest watershed, but he didn't want to do it like everyone else. Instead of starting at the river's headwaters and floating four thousand miles to its mouth at the Atlantic, the choice of most other adventurers, he had the idea of traveling upstream by his own power.

Why?

"If you start from upstream to down, you are sure of where you go," he says. "You always go to the ocean, no choice.

"If you start from mouth of Amazon, you have thousands of chances to go somewhere else. Life is this way, right? Upstream. You don't know which way you go. Sometimes you have a right to choose. Sometimes it's not you. God, or somebody else, choose. I want to test my destiny. The unknown is much funner than downstream."

Kenji had also read a story that captured his imagination, of an ancient stone fort built on a prominent bank of the Amazon. To defend from attack, the tribe built the fort facing the direction in which their potential attackers lived—downstream.

"At least somebody paddled up that time," he says. "I want to feel that invader's feeling. I wanted to see the other view."

After his Sahara and high arctic experiences, Kenji also felt deeply humbled by the forces of nature, especially the wind. He saw how the wind could stop a human in either hot or cold places, and that he was in control of little when traveling on foot. More than once, he envisioned humans as just another organism, no nobler than the desert scorpion (and less adapted to the heat). This fueled in him a desire to live with less, to become like a creature of the jungle. He wanted to test his ability to live off the land as much as he could along the Amazon.

After landing in the craziness of Rio, he boarded a bus and then a boat to Macapa, smack on the Equator and on the vast mouth of the Amazon. At Macapa, the river is wider than the entire length of the Thames. As he flew over the great river delta, he felt a bolt of excitement and fear running through him. At

Photo courtesy Kenji Yoshikawa

twenty-three, he was freer than he had ever been, with months of the unpredict-able before him.

At Macapa, in the thick night air, staring at the river was like looking seaward from the coast of Japan. Only his compass could tell him the whereabouts of the far bank of the Amazon. With the night bugs chattering and the humid air kissing his cheek, Kenji took a deep breath and wondered for the thousandth time if his trek could be done. He planned on covering sixty upstream miles each day (and progressing twelve miles on his "rest" days), for a trip length of sixty days. His plane ticket expired in six months, at which time he would return to Japan.

After a night on the couch of a local he had met, Kenji set out the next day to find a boat. He tried a dugout canoe favored by natives, and promptly rolled the shallow craft over into the river, dunking himself and entertaining the locals, who laughed as this skinny Japanese guy tried to master a craft they were born to.

When one canoe didn't work, he tried lashing two together, which wasn't much better.

As he was testing out a series of dugout canoe combinations in order to find something he could paddle, Kenji noticed the wind picking up at midday. Within an hour, the sky became inky black, rain sheeted down, and waves up to his fore-head churned in the river. He barely got the boat back to shore as the storm raged. He looked out and saw no other boats on the river.

The locals gestured to him that these storms came everyday. Just like the Sahara nomads and the Eskimos of tundra country, the natives shut down when those storms blew in. To dismiss them was to drown.

True to his character, Kenji met people and tried his best to communicate what he was trying to do. In a few days, he had enlisted others in helping him fashion a four-person dugout canoe with wooden outriggers protruding from both sides for stability. He spent more money than he wanted on the canoe, but he figured he would make it up by finding most of his food in the rainforest.

To Kenji's delight, his outriggers worked. He had enough paddling power to overcome the two-mile-per-hour push of the giant river, which brings 20 percent of the world's riverine freshwater to the ocean. The Amazon's flow is so great it allows people on ships miles out in the Atlantic to dip a bottle into the ocean and drink.

After a few hours of paddling upstream on his departure day, Kenji realized a few things. One was that he wasn't moving very fast—a turtle walking on shore could outrun him, he thought. Another revelation: paddling upstream demanded extraordinary concentration and nonstop muscle power.

Photo courtesy Kenji Yoshikawa

"When you stop, get pushed back," he says. "Mentally, that's big impact. You can't rest."

If Kenji was to succeed, he couldn't pause on the river. And he soon found out that pulling to the side offered no refuge. Because the jungle vegetation hung over the shore, his outriggers hit trees and vines before he could reach them with his hands. Though he could sometimes grab a vine for a bit of a rest in an eddy, there was no chance to step foot on land.

Tributaries became his only place of refuge, and he would scout them out every day at about two p.m. He needed to escape the main river before the storms blew in. But even the side streams featured dense vegetation where landing his boat was impossible. The only dependable landing spots became home sites cleared by Native fishermen or wood harvesters.

Losing any of the shyness he once had, Kenji every afternoon sought out those people at their homes. Taken with the odd configuration of his boat and his rudimentary Portuguese, the locals accepted him, allowing him to sleep within their compound. (It was difficult to set up his tent in the jungle, in part because of the uneven, foot-thick mat of fallen leaves and other forest debris.)

While lying in a screened hammock one night, Kenji wiped all other thoughts from his mind and pondered his mission. On his best day, he had gone about twelve miles upriver. That's an impressive number for someone paddling upstream, but it was far short of sixty. On his worst day, he had progressed just three miles. Kenji thought of the entire length of the river, about four thousand miles. Then he did the math.

"Would take four years to finish," he says.

Since he needed to complete his travel in six months to redeem his airline ticket, and he had little money, his heart sank at what he knew would become his second consecutive failed expedition.

Deep in the jungle, Kenji stayed a week with a man named Jose and his family of four. He helped them fish and gather damp wood for the day's smoky fire. He helped Jose process the meat of a sloth or an armadillo. Kenji was impressed with how the family lived, catching just what they would eat each day and gathering just enough wood for the cooking fire.

"People and nature have a very good balance there," he says.

He was happy for the break from paddling. After a few days, water he sipped from a plastic cup no longer gave the bizarre illusion that it was flowing into him, pushing him backward.

During that week, in the silence between halting conversations, Kenji came to a decision.

A few mornings later, he said goodbye to Jose and his family, and shoved his outriggered canoe back into the stream. He pulled hard for the main channel. When he reached it, he let it take him toward the ocean. No more struggling against the flow. He drifted back toward Macapa.

In Macapa, the sounds of honking cars and people and meals that cost money bothered Kenji. He didn't try to sell his boat, as he had planned. Instead, he gathered some supplies and jumped back into the Amazon. He again paddled upstream.

He muscled back to Jose's home. This time, he stayed three months. There, he became that creature of the jungle, eating fish and learning to love the açai plant.

"At first, I don't understand why people love this terrible food," he said of the bitter fruit. "But now it's one of my favorite foods."

He was amazed at life in the jungle, and how one's digestive leavings would disappear within a day, with some other life-form benefiting. Mostly, he remembered the people of the jungle: Jose and his family, and others, like on an afternoon when he made a cold call on a dark tributary to a family of four. They invited him to dinner, which consisted of two fish. Everyone ate portions of the fish until only just one morsel remained, a fish head. Everyone, Kenji knew, wanted to eat the fish head, the oiliest and tastiest part.

"Owner of the house said, 'You are the visitor, you are welcome in my house. You can eat this head,'" Kenji says. "Just a tiny fish head, but that was a special feeling."

After three months in the jungle, Kenji felt the urge to move on. His $300 flight out of South America was one month away, and he wanted to see a landscape that, a few people told him, resembled what he had been seeking.

With most of his money gone, he lived on a dollar a day, hitchhiking across South America, which he found quite productive. A policeman on a motorcycle once even flagged down a truck and advised the driver to give Kenji a ride.

He spent his daily allotment of pesos on food, eating clear soup with a potato for dinner each night. Every three days, he'd add an egg.

"My face looked like I was whistling," he says. "Wasn't whistling. Just skinny."

As in the jungle, people took Kenji in and fed him, rarely giving him their addresses when he asked for them so he could mail them a gift in the future.

When he reached northern Chile and the Atacama Desert—blocked by mountains on each side and fifty times drier than California's Death Valley—Kenji couldn't believe what he was seeing. A red, lifeless landscape that looked just like the photo he had seen on his kitchen table when he was thirteen. He was smitten.

"I see the Martian view. It was exactly Mars here," he says. "Maybe I was traveling just to find this."

He camped in the sand flats and drank in the silence, and once again had time to think. His mind drifted to his last two expeditions and what, to him, stood out.

"I felt like complete loser," he says. "I am nothing, but people were so nice. That had a large impact on my heart."

He reflected on Jose, his wife, and the dark eyes of their two children. The thought of all the people who had picked him up hitchhiking, had taken him in for the night, fed him dinner. All while asking nothing from him in return. After a few more days of exploring the red desert, he came up with another plan, one that would assure he never traveled as a tourist again.

"I wanted to study, to have a goal, to be kind to people who are kind to me," he says. "I can't repay their kindness directly, but if I study and do something in environmental field for the world, I might repay kindness to their children."

While sitting in his tent in South America, Kenji came up with a three-part plan for his life: (1) He would be an expert in some scientific field that would benefit people; (2) He would master English, since it would allow him to reach the most people; and (3) When his life was near its end, he wanted to look back and see that his life had a positive impact on the world.

"Now, twenty-two years later, three targets still the same," Kenji says.

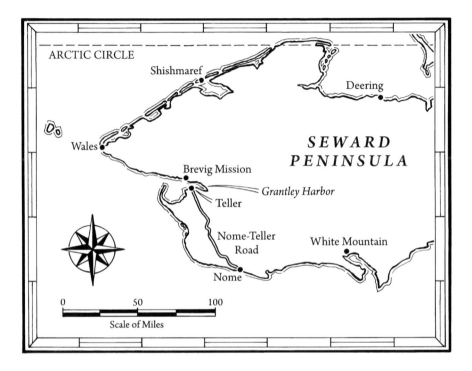

ARCTIC CIRCLE

Shishmaref

Deering

Wales

Brevig Mission

Grantley Harbor

Teller

SEWARD
PENINSULA

Nome-Teller
Road

White Mountain

Nome

0   50   100

Scale of Miles

Chapter Seven

Usually, You Die

On the overcast evening of May 13, 1926, reindeer herders camped on a peninsula north of Teller saw a blob in the sky that matched no images stored in their brains. Over the hills to the north emerged a sharp-edged cloud, shaped like an egg.

"It's a cyclone," said one of the herders, rising from his seat on a driftwood log near a campfire.

"No," said another. "It's a whale!"

The floating apparition drifted closer. Gripped, the herdsmen said nothing. Bulbous and as long as a football field, the mystery object hummed over their heads. They couldn't make sense of it.

Then, from the belly of the beast, came a human voice. "Which way to Nome?"

The four herders were too stunned to reply. The bloated craft floated on.

As the unidentified flying object passed by them, they noticed the word "NORGE" on its flank and several compartments hanging from its belly. Three of these boxes, two to the sides and one at the rear, contained the motors that drove large propellers. The forward gondola had windows and was about the size of a small log cabin.

The herdsmen gaped as the contraption drifted away from them and toward the village of Teller. With their wonder outweighing their fear, they hitched their dogs and started mushing toward the village, four miles away. As their dogs cruised along, they each stole glances upward at the flying machine.

Kay J. Kennedy Aviation Photograph Collection, 1962-69-135,
Archives, University of Alaska Fairbanks

Up in the chilly, cramped main compartment of the dirigible *Norge*, in a combined company of Norwegians and Italians, Roald Amundsen wondered where he was. The fifty-three-year-old Norwegian, recognizable by his steel-blue eyes and nose that curved like an eagle's beak, had a feel for Alaska. Twenty-three years earlier, when his ship the *Gjoa* became the first to traverse the Northwest Passage, Amundsen had traveled by dogsled and ski from Herschel Island, on Canada's northern coast, to Fort Yukon and then on to Eagle. In Eagle, Amundsen sent a telegraph message home, reporting the ship's progress to the outside world. After a comfortable two-month stay in Eagle, he reversed his trip and rejoined his mates on the *Gjoa*. Later, on the *Gjoa's* triumphant journey, Amundsen stopped at Barrow and then Nome.

On his current expedition, during which his North Pole crossing made him the first man to transit both the South and North Poles, he had a few hours before he recognized the coast north of Barrow. Amundsen was ecstatic to have reached Alaska from his starting point at Kings Bay in Spitsbergen.

"Forty-two hours [after leaving Spitsbergen in the *Norge*], we sighted Point Barrow on the north coast of Alaska," Amundsen wrote in *My Life as an Explorer*. "My dream of years had come true! My career as an explorer had been crowned with success in practically the last of the great possible achievements. We had crossed the Arctic Ocean from continent to continent."

That heady tone belied Amundsen's real feelings at the time, as such trium-phant passages are rare in *My Life as an Explorer*, his final book. Amundsen wrote the volume for two reasons: to flesh out his professional résumé and to provide a detailed critique of Italian Umberto Nobile. Nobile was an engineer, the builder of the *Norge* and an ambitious subject of Mussolini's Fascist regime in Italy.

Nobile, a flashy dark figure with perhaps more style than substance, was a nuisance to Amundsen, whose association with the Italian would cost him much of his peace of mind and, a few years later, his life. A major part of that drama had as its setting the small Eskimo village of Teller, Alaska.

Flying over Teller, the aging Norwegian commander hoped the village he saw below was Nome, but his instincts told him otherwise. No matter how his mind lobbied for features he wished to see, something about the town was wrong; the houses were sitting on a large, protected bay. And where was the telegraph mast, Nome's most prominent feature? He explained his arrival in Alaska and the con-fusion it inspired in *My Life as an Explorer*:

> I leave to the reader to imagine, if he can, the thrill we got when our eyes first dis-cerned the north coast of Alaska. On a closer approach, I soon began to make out the familiar landmarks of this coast, which I had first passed twenty years before in the little *Gjoa*. Everything was running smoothly, so we determined to follow the coastline down past Bering Strait and on to Nome. This program did not work out satisfactorily. We soon got into fog and lost our bearings. . . . We proceeded eastward by dead reckoning to avoid the possible necessity of a descent into the waters of the Pacific. After several hours, the fog cleared, and below us on the coast of Alaska we saw a strange settlement.

The *Norge*, after wandering in the fog over northern Alaska, was low on fuel, so Amundsen made the call to land at Teller, even though he wasn't sure where they were. And he knew their failure to go straight to Nome would scuttle the "Rome to Nome" goal of the blimp. But down they went.

Elizabeth Bernhardt Pinson, who lived in Teller and was fourteen years old at the time, described the landing of the *Norge* in her book, *Alaska's Daughter*:

> The engines of the airship were idling, and the propellers just barely turning over. Moving slowly, the dirigible was dropping down and circling low enough that we could see people peering down at us. Then a window opened, and we heard a voice up there in the sky, speaking slowly and distinctly through a megaphone.

"We are going to try to make a landing on the ice."

"That's Amundsen!" Papa said.

"We will drop our mooring ropes, and I want every able-bodied man and boy to come out and grab a hold of them and hang on."

Landing a dirigible was an inexact science, and spectacular crashes, such as the Hindenburg's, were common. There was almost a similar scene in Teller. Pinson wrote of the Norge's graceless descent: "The dirigible bucked and plunged at the end of the ropes, as if the whale it so resembled was trying to free itself of harpoon lines. Suddenly it was pushed by a tremendous gust, smashed down, and rolled over onto the ice. As it struck, it made a noise as if a million tin cans were rattling around inside as the metal girders and catwalks collapsed."

The crew was happy to be done and, being professional explorers, their main concern at the time was delivering word of their accomplishment, as well as telling their loved ones they had survived the trip over the pole. Amundsen had an agreement with U.S. newspapers to deliver them the story, so he searched out the telegraph office in the village.

But the telegraph was broken in Teller, so Amundsen and his co-commander, American Lincoln Ellsworth, hired a boat to take them through the remaining ice cakes and into Nome. There, they worked on stories for several newspapers. At the same time, Amundsen's radioman had repaired the telegraph at Teller. Nobile began sending out press reports in which he called himself a commander of the mission.

Amundsen and Ellsworth both chewed out Nobile when they returned to Teller. After the moody Nobile withdrew to a house in which he was staying, Amundsen thought the issue was dead. He looked forward to reaping the financial benefit of another first.

The issue had not passed away, though, as Theodore Mason wrote in Two Against the Ice: "When Amundsen returned to the United States in November of 1926, he discovered that Nobile was making a lecture tour of the country for his own profit. . . . Amundsen was faced with the task of trying to recover the outstanding debts of the expedition after Nobile had scooped the cream from the news event for himself."

Just a few years before the Norge flight, Amundsen had filed for bankruptcy, describing himself as penniless. With the success of the Norge mission, the fifty-three-year-old had expected that his financial troubles were over, but Nobile had trumped him. The Italian's claims of leadership during

Roald Amundsen. Kay J. Kennedy Aviation Photograph Collection, 1991-98-927, Archives, University of Alaska Fairbanks

Umberto Nobile. Norge Collection, 1981-140-4, Archives, University of Alaska Fairbanks

the mission weighed heavily on Amundsen, who knew he had few adventures left in him.

"Nobile's conduct throughout the expedition from first to last, and his conduct since, have caused me more vexation and humiliation than I can describe," Amundsen wrote in *My Life as an Explorer*, which reads as a cursory account of his feats but then degrades by its conclusion to a full-out attack on Nobile. The book is a memoir of a wounded man, which makes all the more curious what happened next.

Two years after the scrap with Amundsen in Teller, Nobile set off on another dirigible expedition over the far north. In a blimp named *Italia*, Nobile wanted to discover any bodies of land that might exist in the mysterious center of the Arctic Ocean. And he wanted a mission in which he was the undisputed leader.

Nobile and his crew took off from the same Kings Bay base in Spitsbergen as had the *Norge*. He made it to the North Pole, and circled the sea ice at the imaginary point before heading back to Spitsbergen. On the trip back, Nobile ran into raging winds; the dirigible crashed on the sea ice 180 miles north of Kings Bay.

Six crewmen died as the wind swept them away with the deflating blimp, but several, including Nobile and his dog Tintina, survived the crash. The radioman on the mission managed an SOS message, but the men weren't well equipped for life on the sea ice: Nobile, who had suffered a broken arm and leg during the crash, was wearing a sweater and thin pants when the ship went down.

When word spread about the accident, Amundsen was at the Norwegian Yacht Club in Oslo, at a banquet honoring George Wilkins and Carl Eielson, who had made a flight from Barrow to Kings Bay. One could imagine Amundsen indulging in a dark satisfaction at the proof of Nobile's ineptness, but there, amid other men of the same high spirit, Amundsen made a decision. For reasons known only to him, he would mount a rescue mission to help Nobile.

The fifty-four-year-old Amundsen rousted up a rescue team based upon his ability to procure a Latham seaplane from the French. Some historians question whether the Norwegian's assistance was truly needed; at least twenty other planes were also involved in the search. It became a race to see who could find and rescue the survivors first.

Amundsen, a French pilot, a Norwegian pilot, and three French crewmembers took off from the ocean outside Tromso on June 18, 1928. Their radio message of goodbye after takeoff was the last anyone would hear of the first man to see both the South and North Poles. Leaving the northern island, Amundsen and the crew soon disappeared into a maze of sea ice and open leads.

Thinking Amundsen capable of surviving the Arctic longer than the Italians, especially with the round-the-clock daylight of summer solstice, the rescuers who heard of the loss of contact from the Norwegian instead focused their search on Nobile. They would find Amundsen later, they thought, probably with a smile and an understated story of camping on the ice.

Swedish aviators soon rescued Nobile in a controversial fashion, taking the injured commander back to the safety of a base ship with his dog before the rest of his men. His failure to stay with the ship until his team was evacuated sullied his reputation.

Nobile endured four decades longer than did Amundsen. He lived to the age of ninety-three, dying in Italy in 1978.

Somewhere out there on the northern ice pack, Amundsen perished in June or July of 1928. Norwegian fishermen later found parts of the fuel tank and a patched float from the seaplane, which suggested that Amundsen and crew might have tried to use the float as a life raft. Amundsen was fifty-four when he disappeared.

Just before that fateful trip, Amundsen had spoken with an Italian reporter about the mission of search and rescue for Nobile. "If you only knew how splendid it is up there! That's where I want to die; and I only hope death will come to me chivalrously, that it will overtake me in the fulfillment of a high mission, quickly, without suffering."

On the same land that Amundsen took his final steps, the island of Spitsbergen, Kenji studied for his master's degree, examining, mostly by drilling and shoveling, what he calls the most beautiful expression of frozen water, a dome of land called a pingo. While there, digging pits in frozen ground, he read narratives by Amundsen and Fridtjof Nansen, who used the islands as a training ground for grand northern adventures.

Kenji admires Amundsen and his feats, especially the Northwest Passage trip and a winter on the ice Kenji would later emulate. But he also sees the trappings of becoming a professional adventurer with no backup plan.

"If just explorer, when you get old, not as good anymore," he says. "Usually, you die [on an expedition]."

Fridtjof Nansen, a hero of Kenji's who discovered so much about the Arctic Ocean in the *Fram*, later satisfied his challenge-hungry soul by becoming a diplomat. Nansen earned a Nobel Prize at age sixty-two for his work finding and organizing the delivery of food to millions of people dying in the Russian famine of 1921–1922.

"He wanted to make it to Antarctica, but he knew he was too old," Kenji says of Nansen. "Still, he had good time doing other things."

∎ ∎ ∎

The sun is shining on a spring day in Teller so brilliant it makes the slow, squeaky snow of winter seem years in the past. We pull up in front of the school after three hours of snowmachining a gravel road buried under ten feet of wind-sculpted, kidney-rattling snow. Teller is a hybrid village—a Native settlement on a road system. Getting off our machines, we see the familiar evidence of two cultures bumping together: a giant metal-sided school and, a few hundred feet away, two dead seals frozen into a snowdrift.

Teller, somewhat nondescript as far as Alaska villages go, has an exploration history that goes beyond Amundsen's final triumph. Captain James Cook, just

months before his death by knife in Hawaii, sought the refuge of Grantley Harbor, the same place the *Norge* landed. Kenji himself has spent months there, on his first great voyage by sea. Remembering that as he cruises into town, Kenji wonders if any of the teenagers we pass were the young children he spoke with fifteen years ago, and if they remember the Japanese man with the orange boat who anchored there in the 1990s.

Today, within minutes of our arrival at the school, Kenji is speaking with the principal and receiving permission to drill a permafrost observatory on a prominent hill, where graves are dug into permafrost and where people park their snowmachines and four-wheelers when the forecast calls for a storm surge. Most of Teller sits just a few feet above sea level.

As we prepare to drill another permafrost observatory, Kenji discovers something that disturbs him: his big blue drill isn't working.

"Might have bounced too much," he says, frowning.

The ride from Nome included miles-long stretches of sastrugi—rock-hard snow with gouged-out gaps that leave your machine suspended in midair, until it smashes down on another plate. It's like riding over an ocean with frozen waves.

The sleds absorbed a few dozen body slams over the tough stretches, and the case protecting the drill cracked. This allowed some snow to reach the drill, and

that pounding may have worked the snow into its interior. Whatever has happened, Kenji's most important tool isn't working.

"You drill frost tube," Kenji tells Tohru. "I go to Brevig Mission and back, check out site over there. Let the big drill dry out in classroom."

Kenji zooms away to Brevig Mission while Tohru and I set up the small-diameter frost tube drill on the high spot in Teller. We watch Kenji disappear toward Brevig along a trail cut across sea ice. In the cold blue sky, we see no blimps in the air above him—an image that would be as bizarre today as it was in 1926.

. . .

After finding Mars in South America, a tanned, lean, twenty-three-year-old Kenji caught his cheap flight back to Tokyo and made his way back to school in Okinawa. Tapped out from traveling, he poured his energy into finding several jobs to pay for school and his next series of adventures.

Always looking for ways to earn the most money in the shortest period of time, Kenji once talked his way into being a salesman for a cosmetics company. He was an unlikely dealer of makeup. With his high forehead and somewhat intimidating look, some of his friends had nicknamed him Frankenstein. But Kenji was fearless in his approach. With a briefcase full of cosmetics, he hustled from department store to department store, pitching his wares. Kenji became so successful that the manager of the cosmetics company challenged him. The manager was falling far short of his sales goals. Could Kenji sell three million yen worth (about $30,000)?

In Hokkaido, Kenji set up in a large department store, enlisting two lovely young women as assistants. He then employed a high-pressure sales pitch, telling passing women that he would only sell cosmetics for the last ten minutes of the hour, at special prices, and they would receive free gifts if they were there for the event. "Super special sale," he said. "Last one of the year. Miss it and you miss your chance."

For the other fifty minutes of each hour he was there, Kenji retired to a back room and drank tea with the girls, while at the cosmetics counter frenzied women told their friends about the sale and the gifts. When Kenji reemerged, women were queued up at the counter. The girls helped him with sales, not believing how far the lines snaked through the store. In three days, he sold $30,000 worth.

Kenji also started his own business: taking photographs with a camera he suspended from a self-made kite. He snapped photos from hundreds of feet in the air and sold them to companies that otherwise would have spent a lot more hiring helicopter or aircraft pilots to do the same thing.

In Hokkaido, he heard people complaining about mosquitoes, and the bulb of opportunity again lit in his brain. He noticed the repellants they were using didn't include DEET. Knowing he could buy robust, DEET-rich repellant from the base exchanges of the U.S. military posts in Okinawa, Kenji was soon filling a duffle bag with plastic bottles of repellant and carrying it to Hokkaido. He sold it in northern Japan to owners of outdoors shops; clerks in the U.S. stores on Okinawa would stockpile bottles for him, putting them aside until Kenji showed up. "Whatever they have, I buy all," he says.

His sleeping mat again grew lumpy from the yen notes he was stowing. He soon began withdrawing them to help prepare to see another barren earthen landscape—the Greenland ice sheet. He had a desire to walk across the ice cap, doing science along the way. "I like to walk forever, to the horizon," he says. "I want to see my track back of me continue to the horizon. Like the Sahara." True to his nature, he was thinking one step ahead as he prepared for Greenland; his main objective was the planet's great frontier of ice and snow—Antarctica.

Kenji's experience in Resolute Bay taught him many things about the cold, mostly that he had a lot to learn. One thing he remembered was that products he could buy in a sporting goods store were not good in the cold. So he pored

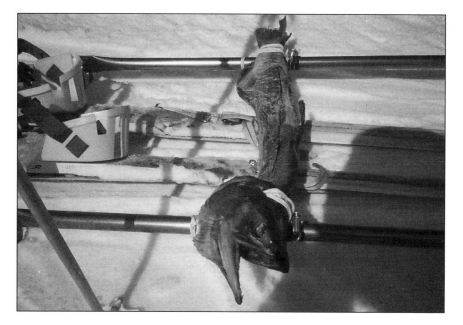

Photo courtesy Kenji Yoshikawa

through journals of adventurers, among them *Farthest North* by Nansen and Amundsen's *The North West Passage*. He visited museums displaying their old equipment, saw what worked, and went about inventing some of his own.

"I am not good engineer," he says. "Better to study others, read what kind of sleds they use, like longer ones for coast, shorter for forest."

Having made the mistake of building a tippy sled on skis for his attempt on the magnetic North Pole, Kenji studied the sledges of the old explorers. For the wind-carved surfaces of both Greenland and Antarctica, Kenji knew his sled needed a few features—its center of gravity had to be low, he wanted it the perfect height for him sit on and relax in a landscape without logs or rocks, and it needed to be large enough to crawl into in case of emergency.

He constructed what would become one of his favorite inventions, a sled with two parallel chambers running its length. He designed the grooves to fit what would later become known as the Yoshikawa Biscuit, his main food source. With advice from canoe builders, Kenji decided to make his sled of four layers of fiberglass, then two layers of Kevlar, a layer of carbon, and a final layer of "s-glass," a high-strength mixture of compounds often used in aircraft.

"Sled never break," Kenji says. "This is my proudest sled. Almost five thousand kilometer, never tip over."

Kenji's sled also featured an edible component. Wanting an emergency food source that was also useful in the structure of the sled, Kenji asked a friend who worked in a fish-packing company to dry out several whole salmon. Kenji then attached the rigid fish between the fiberglass poles that extended from the sled to the waist belt. The fish added stability to the rigging and, in a pinch, could keep a person alive for a few days. But the biological sled component later proved to be a pain, Kenji says, because parts of salmon that touched the snow in bright sunshine would turn mushy.

"Every time stop, can't touch pole to ground," he says. "This is highest care. Terrible."

Kenji and his travel companions would rely for sustenance on another of his innovations, the Yoshikawa Biscuit. In reading about the polar explorers, Kenji took notes on what they were eating. He jotted down what would be his ideal for

Photos courtesy Kenji Yoshikawa

a long trip walking on skis over snow and ice. Packed with energy and relatively lightweight, fatty foods are great for winter travel, but even those accustomed to high-fat diets get constipated when they dramatically boost their intake. Carbohydrates taste good, but their weight makes them one of the most inefficient foods in an arctic environment. In the end, Kenji looked to his memories of the Native foods that had kept him warm around Resolute Bay.

"Inuit eat lots of seal oil," he says. "About 34 percent of their diet is fat."

Kenji then sought to develop a food that contained about 34 percent fat, which he figured as the upper level anyone could stomach. He remembered reading about how Japanese researchers had developed a biscuit with no flour at an Antarctica station in 1957. He decided to make his own.

Into one patty the size of a giant cheeseburger, Kenji combined egg yolk, powdered milk, butter, sugar, oatmeal, soybean powder, Parmesan cheese, mashed potatoes, sesame seeds, a few other nuts, and sometimes hot chocolate. Each biscuit—34 percent fat, 14 percent protein, and 52 percent carbs—provided two thousand calories, about the same as two Big Macs and a large order of fries.

"Just two biscuits per day, you don't need other food," he says.

Armed with rows of biscuits in his salmon-buttressed sled, Kenji made two trips to Greenland. On the first, he wanted to cross the ice sheet alone, starting from Ilimanaq on the west coast. He spent a week going out and back on the ice, and then returned to the village where all one hundred residents were either relatives or friends. He stayed a few months, finding a place in the hearts of village elders when he pulled in their heavy fishnets twice a day.

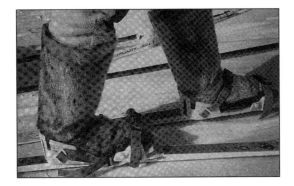

Photo courtesy Kenji Yoshikawa

His contacts in the village proved valuable just a few months before he and a team of two others planned to ski to the South Pole. The trio traveled to Kangerlussuaq, also on the west coast, and prepared for a shakedown trip on skis across Greenland just as Nansen had done almost a century earlier. Kenji's goal was to test equipment on the ice cap, choosing what might work for Antarctica.

The three partners on the ski—Tetsuya Sano, Masayuki Matsubara, and Kenji—pulled the sleds weighed down by the biscuits. They wore kamiks, seal-skin shoes they fixed to their Fischer E-99 skis with a binding that attached the boot to the ski with a thin strip of plastic, which somehow didn't break in the cold. Most of their gear would get a thumbs-up for use in Antarctica.

Kenji tested everything on Greenland: he used a kite to suspend an antenna wire to increase his radio's range. Team members collaborated on a smaller replica of the Nansen cooker, a pot with four exhaust vents that allow thawing of ice around the sides of the pot while liquid warms within. Next to their cooker, he fired up the Swedish Optimus stove, which hasn't changed in design since 1888. He chose their variation of Nansen's design for Antarctica. "Uses two-thirds the kerosene of regular cooker," Kenji says.

Weight was the number-one issue regarding their sleds. With nowhere to refuel or to get food, they had to carry everything; fuel accounted for one quarter of the weight they carried over the Greenland ice plateau in their sleds. One half of their load was biscuit. The sleds were heavier than they were, almost two hundred pounds, and were dreadfully slow, but they had shaved their poundage as much as they dared.

The first few days in Greenland, the partners slogged fewer than ten miles each day through snow that wasn't as firm as they had expected. They powered

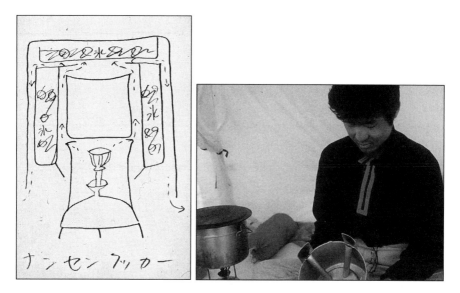

Nansen's cooker melts ice chunks in side chambers while boiling water over a flame. Photos courtesy Kenji Yoshikawa.

on. The biscuit seemed sufficient to keep a man moving, if not leave him craving more.

On the crystalline mornings he and his mates woke in their tent pitched atop thousands of feet of ice, Kenji thought of Nansen. Early on in the trip, he knew that they were not covering enough miles to be able to cross the three-hundred-mile width of the ice cap. But Nansen failed many times, Kenji thought, and even though most other people would regard skiing across one of the world's great masses of ice as the trip of a lifetime, on Greenland he felt like an actor in a dress rehearsal.

Antarctica was the larger goal, and when the Greenland expedition ended at a NATO base with the team having fallen short of their crossing, Kenji was content. He and the team members, who would accompany him to Antarctica in two short months, had survived the trip without major frostbite or other debilitating injuries, and they had learned enough, it seemed. As they rode in a helicopter from the NATO base to the coast of Greenland, each young man's thoughts drifted to what it might be like to walk on skis across the world's largest ice sheet, home to the coldest air ever recorded on Earth, minus 129 degrees.

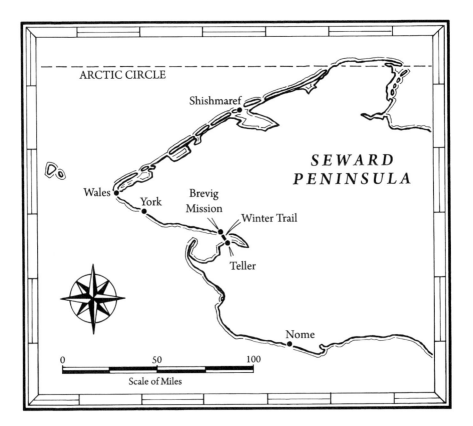

ARCTIC CIRCLE

Shishmaref

SEWARD
PENINSULA

Wales
York
Brevig
Mission
Winter Trail
Teller

Nome

0   50   100
Scale of Miles

Chapter Eight

Secret of the Permafrost

On a stinging gray day, we ride our machines past crooked white crosses on a small hill. The graveyard marks the entrance to Brevig Mission, population 276. We pass an extra-large cross, close to seven feet tall, but don't think about it as we head for the school. That cross marks the burial site of the seventy-two people who died of the flu in 1918. Because of the chaos and sickness at the time (and the fact that only eight villagers remained, most of them children), there was no time or energy for individual plots.

Tired from the day's travel from Nome and the frost-tube drilling in Teller, Tohru and I stake out a place in the teachers' lounge to spread our sleeping bags. There isn't much room between tables and chairs, but the narrow spaces lend coziness to the room; the darkness and the smell of burnt coffee are a pleasant contrast to the blowing snow outside. Kenji, who was talking to a teacher the last time we saw him, walks into the room carrying his blue Bosch drill. He looks sad, depressed, like we've never seen him on this trip.

"Drill still broken," he says. "If can't fix, trip is over."

He spreads a sheet of construction paper over a table and lays the drill upon it with the gentleness he would show a newborn. Kenji frowns and blows into the vents of the drill, which sprout beads of water as the heat of the room thaws the instrument. His big drill—injured from our lumpy ride on the wind-tortured snow between Teller and Nome—is one of the few items he can't replace out here. We could probably find anything else, including a generator, at the village

Mass grave in Brevig Mission

stores. But the lack of his drill, which is the perfect size and torque for his three-foot bits designed to chew through frozen soil, is a showstopper.

Kenji doesn't fear mechanical things and will find someone to help him should the drill be dead, but the downtime is not built into his schedule. He carries more equipment inside the teachers' lounge and hopes for the best.

One hour later, Kenji is happy. After the heat and dryness of the Brevig Mission School penetrated the plastic case of the forty-pound electric drill, a liquid short circuit between electric components dried up and vanished. He pulled the trigger and the drill spun.

His big blue drill works, and we are headed outside, on the same day we have seen Lance Mackey eat breakfast in Nome, snowmachined seventy bumpy miles to Teller, met with the teacher in Teller, received permission to drill, found the big drill wasn't working, drilled a frost tube observatory in Teller with the smaller drill, spoke with Teller students, snowmachined a few more miles here, met with the Brevig principal, got permission to drill in Brevig, and waited for Kenji's drill to heal.

It's nine p.m. and, in late March, the sun won't set for about two hours. And Kenji won't shut 'er down while daylight is burning.

"Ready?" he asks, drill case in hand.

Kenji picks a spot just west of town, next to a fish rack draped with two musk oxen hides, hooves still attached. Three Native boys, who look cold in their sweatshirts and Brevig Mission Huskies wool hats, watch Kenji work. In an hour, he

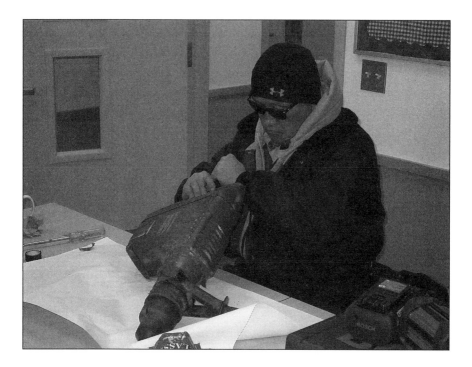

is done with another observatory. The temperature about six feet down is about thirty degrees, showing that permafrost is indeed present in Brevig Mission. But another event had already confirmed that. Six feet is about the same depth that gold miners, hired from Nome in January 1919, thawed with steam points the ground on the east end of town. Into this icy tomb, sixty days after the people of Brevig died, the miners dragged seventy-two bodies large and small. Returning to equilibrium, the ground froze again after the miners closed the grave. The flu victims themselves became permafrost, defined as any dirt or anything else in the ground that remains frozen for two or more years.

. . .

Anno Domini 1918 was not Alaska's finest year. The gold rushes that had attracted so many people north had stalled, and then dried up. Most of the adventure seekers sniffed out prospects elsewhere.

In 1918, Alaska's population would have filled Yankee Stadium. But the crowd was filing out. At least ten thousand people had left since 1910, leaving about fifty-five thousand in the territory. In addition to the loss of gold seekers, another good part of the exodus was due to the desperate opportunity the U.S. Army provided near the end of World War I. Alaska's territorial Governor, Thomas Riggs, estimated that 12 percent of Alaska's population had joined the army. Most of those Alaskans were fortunate to be somewhere else as a deadly microscopic invader steamed its way toward Alaska's ports.

The "Spanish flu" of 1918 infected 28 percent of the United States population, killing 675,000 of them. The virus infected one-third of the world's population. While there are no accurate counts of that horrific event less than a century ago, at least fifty million and possibly as many as one hundred million people died worldwide. With the size of its population figured in, Alaska was one of the hardest places hit.

The splendid isolation Alaskans enjoy today when driving from Tok to Glennallen without passing another car was what in 1918 doomed a few thousand. Remote populations, like all the people living in Alaska in 1918, are vulnerable to new, nasty viruses. Shut off from the germs of the larger world, Alaskans—especially the Natives, with their generations of living apart—developed little or no resistance. The distance and cold that had served Alaskans so well in avoiding diseases before 1918 became their worst enemy when the flu reached Alaska's ports on the lips of people riding steamships.

Despite protocol in which Seattle officials checked all people boarding the Nome-bound *Victoria* for flu symptoms, and a five-day shipboard quarantine before passengers could walk off the gangplank onto the Seward Peninsula, the virus was lurking undetected within at least one person on board, probably more. Soon after the quarantine ended and the travelers mingled with the locals, the flu struck Nome.

"Within days an appallingly large proportion of the inhabitants of [Nome] and its satellite villages of Eskimos were sick and dying," wrote Alfred Crosby in *America's Forgotten Pandemic: The Influenza of 1918.* "In Nome, nearly everything that could go wrong did so. The *Victoria*, which apparently brought Spanish influenza, was the last ship of the season, and therefore Nome and the whole Seward Peninsula had to fight the flu without any assistance.

"Spanish influenza did to Nome and the Seward Peninsula what the Black Death did to fourteenth-century Europe."

Within a few weeks, 80 out of 150 people died in Teller. In the corner of Nome where the Natives lived, 162 people died in eight days. Wales had a population of 310 before the flu arrived, 140 after. The next village to the east, the former

Teller graveyard

gold-mining camp of York, still on USGS maps, is now a true ghost town, having lost every single resident to the flu.

Two thousand people died in Alaska, including almost 10 percent of the Native population. The scene was grim, as Alaska Governor Riggs wrote in his annual report to the Secretary of the Interior. "I doubt if similar conditions existed anywhere in the world—the intense cold of the arctic days, the long distances to be traveled by dog team, the living children huddled against their parents already being gnawed by wolfish dogs."

Perhaps arriving with the cough of a mail carrier who arrived by dogsled, on November 15, 1918, the flu virus invaded Brevig Mission, the next village on the trail east from York. Five days later, seventy-two of eighty villagers were dead. As in other villages, the survivors, once they regained their strength (which took two months in the case of Brevig), commissioned the burial of those seventy-two people in a mass grave. That mound of disturbed tundra, and a woman within it, was to solve a deadly mystery almost a century later.

■ ■ ■

Though he suspected that his unusual quest might be newsworthy, Johan Hultin did not call any reporters before he went to visit Brevig Mission in 1997. The retired pathologist from San Francisco knew in his gut the village held the secret of the Spanish flu of 1918. But he also knew that retrieving it would be difficult.

He bought a ticket from San Francisco to Nome for August 1997. When in Nome he would purchase another for the forty-five-minute flight to Brevig. He did not tell the village elders he was coming. Some things, like the unearthing of long-dead relatives, are best addressed face-to-face.

As Hultin's flight banked over the small village, he saw the familiar graveyard on the hill by the small lagoon. He thought briefly of the last time he was there, and how much his life had changed in those four-plus decades. He said a short prayer that the ground around Brevig, especially the exposed surface of the graveyard, was still frozen a few feet beneath the surface, as it had been when he was there in 1951.

Back in the 1950s, Hultin was studying microbiology at the University of Iowa. A native of Sweden who challenged himself with his life choices, he was the sort who followed the pull of adventure. When Hultin was twenty-four, a few months before school at Iowa began, he wanted to travel the new land with his new wife, Gunvor. Not sure how long they would be in America, they would see as much as they could. In a 1947 Studebaker Hultin borrowed from a generous aunt, they visited each of the Lower Forty-eight states and all but two provinces in Canada. They then pointed the car north and drove up the Alaska Highway, which had just opened to nonmilitary traffic.

In Fairbanks, Hultin drove to the university, where he and Gunvor stayed in a dorm room while students were away on summer break. There, he had the good fortune of meeting Otto Geist, a German paleontologist and museum collector who happened to need an assistant for the summer. In exchange for the help, Geist offered the Hultins free lodging at the university. Johan accepted before the words had left Geist's mouth.

The Hultins traveled throughout the northern part of the state with Geist, noticing that the villagers seemed to be quite happy at the arrival of Geist, treating him like a brother or a favorite uncle. Witnessing this, Johan knew he had hooked up with a special person.

After a summer of fun and adventurous travel to places few people had seen in Alaska, the first bite of winter slowed Geist's travels. The departure of geese in formation and return of students to the university nudged Johan and Gunvor southward. When the Hultins rolled out of Fairbanks, Johan felt the pangs that come with leaving a place that has changed your life in a good way.

They drove the Studebaker back down the Alaska Highway, then south to Johan's aunt in Arizona. After saying thank you, Johan and Gunvor then caught a train back to the Midwest, arriving in Iowa a few days later. There, Johan embarked with a fresh spirit on his studies, becoming fascinated with tiny organisms that wreaked havoc on the delicate yet resilient machine of the human body.

A fine student, Johan once had a meeting with a visiting professor who gave a lecture during lunch. The professor spoke of how no one had ever identified the virus responsible for the 1918 flu. He also mentioned a possible method of finding it. "The virus may remain in the tissue of peoples from the far north who might be buried in a very cold place," he said. *Epiphany*, Hultin thought. Right then, right there, he had his mission in life. He didn't know how or when it would materialize, but he knew he would play some part in identifying what he calls "the most lethal organism in the history of man."

The first time Hultin visited Brevig Mission, he was with his friend Geist and two Iowa researchers. The year was 1951. With the help of Geist, Hultin received permission from village elders to dig into the mass grave; his plan was to gather live flu virus from the lungs of the victims.

It was slow work: building fires on the surface of the mass grave, letting the coals die, digging into the thawed soil, removing it, and building another fire. It took two days. But the men reached the bodies, and Hultin removed tissue from four of them. The men closed the grave and replaced the two wooden crosses.

Hultin returned with the samples to a lab in Iowa, trying to revive the virus with every method known to science at the time. He failed, and he thought the mystery of the Spanish flu would never be solved. *Oh well*, he thought. *At least I gave it my best.*

The story, however, was as persistent as Hultin's interest. In 1997, Hultin, then seventy-two and living in San Francisco, read a story in *Science* about a molecular pathologist in Washington, D.C., working on samples of flu-tainted tissue from two Civil War soldiers. He read that the researcher, who felt he was close to identifying the virus, lamented not having any more samples. Epiphany number two.

Hultin read the article again, and again, and then wrote a letter to the pathologist, Jeffery Taubenberger of the Armed Forces Institute of Pathology. *I think I can get you a sample of the Spanish flu virus. I am not crazy. Here is my story. . . .*

Landing in Brevig Mission in August 1997, the seventy-two-year-old Hultin first went to Brian Crockett, a Lutheran pastor in the village, and explained how he wanted to exhume the grave again, for what might be the good of all mankind. If the virus was still there, researchers could fingerprint it, then make a vaccine for it. No one needed to die again because of it.

Crockett listened with great interest. He picked up the phone and called Rita Olanna, a member of the village council in Brevig. After Hultin pled his case to Olanna, she got the village council to agree to his unusual request. Also, she asked, would he like four young men to help him dig?

Hultin thawed the grave with the heat of a willow fire, the same technique he employed in 1951. They opened a hole six feet wide and twenty-eight feet long.

He uncovered skeletons—the bodies had completely decomposed and had no useful tissue for him. That discouraged Hultin, but he reminded himself that his labor in 1951 exposed the top bodies to warmer soil than would have been present at an undisturbed site. He pressed on until he saw her, a woman he called "Lucy." Her body was relatively intact.

"I sat on a pail—turned upside down—and looked at her," Hultin told Gina Kolata, the author of *Flu: The Story of the Great Influenza Pandemic of 1918 and the Search for the Virus that Caused It.* "Then I saw it. She was an obese woman; she had fat in her skin and around her organs and that served as a protection from the

occasional short-term thawing of permafrost. Those on either side of her were not obese and they had decayed."

With surgical tools, he removed Lucy's lungs. He kept them frozen to preserve them, and shipped them to Taubenberger in D.C. In 2005, Taubenberger and his colleagues used the samples to reconstruct the virus, determining that it originated in birds and mutated to infect people. Researchers have now developed a vaccine. The Spanish flu will never again infect remote villages, nor anywhere else with access to modern medicine.

"The only sample we [had was] there because the elders of Brevig Mission let me go back into the grave again," Hultin said. "They gave us the opportunity to do something good. Not just for themselves, but for the whole world."

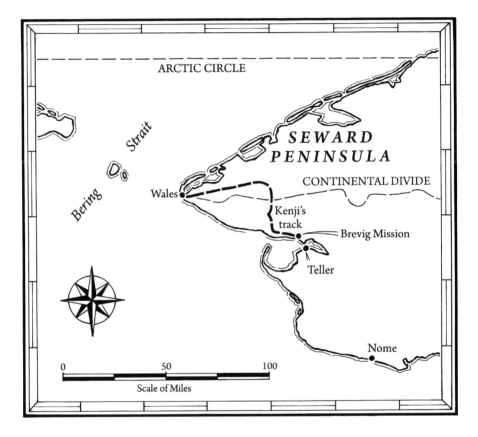

ARCTIC CIRCLE

Bering Strait

Do

SEWARD
PENINSULA

CONTINENTAL DIVIDE

Wales

Kenji's
track

Brevig Mission

Teller

Nome

0   50   100

Scale of Miles

Chapter Nine

To the End of the Earth

N o tracks of human foot or machine are pressed into the snow just west of Brevig Mission. The village of Wales, at the jutting tip of the windburned nose of the Seward Peninsula, is about seventy miles from Brevig, but few villagers motor there during the winter. If someone needs to reach Wales, they take a snowmachine or a four-wheeler to the airstrip, park it, and step aboard a twin-engine plane.

But Kenji has a snowmachine, and that's how he will get to Wales. During our night in Brevig, he asked every passing person wearing oil-stained Carhartts for directions to Wales. Some told him the trail was a relatively straight shot along the sea ice, hugging the coast and passing York (which is still on the map despite being without people) before heading inland at Tin City. The USGS maps seem to confirm this, with dotted lines along the coast labeled "WINTER TRAIL."

As we buy gas on another spring day painted battleship gray, Kenji asks a question of the Native man selling us fuel.

"You know trail to Wales?"

"There is none," the man says, the wind lifting the flaps of his fur hat, exposing his ears to zero-degree air, the bite of which makes him squint. "Come inside the store. I'll show you."

The man selling gas also runs the store. Inside the fluorescent-lit, windowless structure, he collects Kenji's money for topping our tanks and a few jugs of fuel we'll carry but probably won't need.

The man unfolds a map on the counter. He looks like a dad, like a husband, like a basketball coach and a seal hunter. He points the way to Kenji, running his finger over the map. "Can't go on the sea ice," he says. "It's drifted offshore. There's no ice just beyond the [Brevig] lagoon."

Outside, visibility is poor; it's the flat latex finish that makes your snowmachine rumble over bumps before you see them and wish your spine had shock absorbers. If we had tried the sea-ice route, our iron dogs might have deposited us into the ocean. But Kenji never stops asking questions.

The storekeeper gives Kenji advice on the all-land route to Wales. It's a seventy-five-mile trip up and over the Continental Divide and out to the Bering Strait, one of several places in Alaska where, on a good day, you can indeed see Russia. Kenji squints at the map for a few minutes, asks more questions, and memorizes the route. The Don River is the watershed we'll drive up after getting off the lagoon west of town.

Out on the ice of Brevig Lagoon, Kenji leans his machine into a right turn up the Don River. The stream is a subtle feature, a slight sink of the landscape that's hard to make out in this white-on-white world. Kenji will later say he knew to turn there because he counted creeks on his way out of Brevig and matched them to his memory of the map. At creek number three, he turned uphill.

We cruise up Don River until the hill splits the frozen waterway into a Y. We take the right fork and cruise for a few minutes. Then Kenji loops back to Tohru and me.

"Wrong way," he says. Then he turns left through a flattish snowfield and motors on.

"How'd he know where we are?" I ask Tohru.

"I don't know," he says. "I think maybe because the valley started curving too much to the right."

We follow Kenji through a few gullies and back to the main branch of the Don River and head northward. Within an hour, and without much drama except the sensation that our thumbs are easing off the throttles, we cross an invisible lake that marks the Continental Divide. We'll drop a bit and follow parallel to the imaginary line until we reach Cape Prince of Wales, the spot where the ridgepole of North America touches saltwater for the first time since Panama.

Crossing the divide is like taking a white plastic bag off our heads; we are out of the frozen mist and, on the northern side, into a sunny day that will soon allow us to view another continent. We can see far enough to notice three musk oxen scooting their butts together to face outward in their defensive shield position (which works great against wolves but doesn't do much to repel bullets, which is why the last Alaska musk ox was shot off the Kandik River in the 1890s, to be replaced a few decades later by a hardy group of transplants from Greenland). Their pasted-on horns make them look like they've slicked down their hair to perform in a barbershop quartet. We cruise by the three giants in a scene that could be the Pleistocene, were it not for the tang of two-stroke fuel in the air.

We are Out There, cutting our own track across the top of the Seward Peninsula, where our frozen exhaust will someday trickle to the Chukchi Sea. (The snow we traveled on before crossing the divide will in a few months melt and flow to the Bering Sea.) We are about thirty miles from the nearest people, who live in Wales. There are lonelier spots in Alaska (like the island of St. Matthew in the Bering Sea, two hundred miles from the nearest village), but none down there in the Lower Forty-eight, as Gary Hart wrote in *Hawk's Rest*, a book about Yellowstone Park. "Out of the million square miles of basin, range, peaks and prairies that compose the interior West, the farthest it's possible to be from a road is a trifling 28 miles."

We descend to the coast, Kenji cutting a path of blue shadows into unbroken snow. The sleds behind the snowmachines rhythmically go *bam* as we drag them over sastrugi, assuring the musk oxen will continue strolling the other way. In the distance, the vastness of the Chukchi Sea and its nothingness stretches more than one thousand miles over the pole to Franz Josef Land. The great ocean is recognizable by the wind-hardened snow, scratched only by polar bears, foxes, and ravens.

Soon, the stegosaurus spine of black rock that signals the entrance to Wales is before us. We merge into an on-ramp of machine-packed snow, the first since Brevig, and follow the track to town.

We drive around the hogback of rock, past the towering mechanical daisies with petals that once cut the village's reliance on diesel, until the wind generators broke and the money to fix them ran out. We ride past the listing wooden crosses of the graveyard near the beach. To our right, twenty-right miles offshore, is the molar of rock that is Little Diomede Island (USA). The island is superposed on the silhouette of Big Diomede Island (Russia, 2.5 miles from Little Diomede). The Russians are closer than the nearest movie theater. During the cold war years, armed soldiers guarded the coasts of both islands in what must have been some of the most boring duty of the Reagan years. At the moment, Wales is quiet. The Russians seem to be of little threat.

We cruise into town on its only street, past buildings that make Shaktoolik's drifting problem look minor. The banks reach the roofs of some houses, and one can't help but wonder if the sun has enough punch at this latitude to melt the snow during the summer, or if the drifts might form a man-assisted glacier, one that will endure until the cold air of winter returns and then survive the year after that, and another few years, until the snow at the bottom gets pressed into deep blue ice.

In this village of 150 people, one of the smaller communities on a peninsula of small communities, Kenji crawls his machine over hills and valleys to the Wales school, which is as big as a suburban health club but is in danger of being smothered by billions of snow crystals the size of pin heads.

With one little hitch back there before the Continental Divide, Kenji has cut his own trail to another village in new country. As a follower in the bouncing caravan, today is the day that most impresses me—that nearly seamless navigation through trail-less country—but maybe I shouldn't be surprised. He has had lots of practice.

*   *   *

At twenty-eight, Hiroshi Onishi was lean and fluid, a born leader and an alpinist whose accomplishments were demanding attention from climbers even outside Japan. The Tokyo resident had waded through soupy sea ice to reach the North Pole on foot with British explorer Robert Swan in May 1989. Five months later, he reached the summit of Mt. Everest. The next year, he gritted out another Himalaya climb up the even more technical 27,762-foot Makulu.

The gifted young man had gone to the same university as Naomi Uemura, whose body still rests somewhere high on Denali. On North America's highest peak, in 1984, Uemura was trying to be the first person to climb the mountain in winter all by himself. Uemura was a specialist at accomplishing things without a partner; he paddled the Amazon alone, reached the North Pole solo, and, in 1970, became the first to summit Denali by himself. Uemura made radio contact with a pilot near the mountain on that clear February day, but he didn't answer a radio call the next day, nor the days after. None of the hundreds of climbers who have walked Denali's slopes since have found his body.

Onishi had a desire to do something even his idol Uemura had not done. He wanted to be the first man to leave his footprints on the three great extremities of the Earth: its highest point and both of its frigid poles. Having accomplished two of those goals, Onishi was planning for the third—a ski/walk across Antarctica, ending at the South Pole. After meeting Kenji through a professor who knew of Kenji's work and travels in Greenland, Onishi asked Kenji if he would go with him, as the member of the expedition who performed most of the scientific research.

Onishi was pleased to have recruited Kenji for the Antarctica trip before he flew off for an attempt at the highest unclimbed mountain in the world, Tibet's Namcha Barwa. Almost two years to the day after summiting Everest, Onishi was leading a team of Japanese and Chinese climbers through the deep snow on Namcha Barwa. Without warning, a wall of snow fractured above him. His climbing partners were spared, but Onishi was exposed in the chute and had a few terrible seconds to contemplate the slabs of rock-hard snow the size of cars that were descending upon him. By the time his partners could extract him from snow that had sintered into concrete, Onishi was not breathing.

Kenji was in Okinawa when he learned of his friend's death. In shock, he drove to the beach, got out, and sprinted on the sand until his toes burned. He walked back to his van (also his home at the time, where he slept and studied) and lit a cigarette, trying to make sense of the news. *Maybe he's still alive. Maybe the report was in error; people can survive after being under snow for a short period; Onishi-san was tougher than most.*

But the news reports were true, and Kenji and the remaining expedition members had a decision to make. After all that dreaming and preparation, should they cancel the trip to Antarctica? Kenji called his friends from the Greenland expedition—climber and beer-company salesman Masayuki Matsubara and Tetsuya Sano.

In a hot room in Tokyo, where Kenji had moved from Okinawa to make trip preparations easier, they drank Sapporo beers in honor of their friend and spoke late into the night. In the early-morning hours, they decided the best way to honor Onishi was by trying to complete the mission. Their new leader would be the oldest guy, at twenty-nine, also the person with the most experience in alien environments: Kenji.

The team faced an immediate challenge: with Onishi gone, several sponsors for the trip backed out. A trip to Antarctica is expensive, beginning with flights to Chile and then to Antarctica, and there was no way the three men—plus a support team of two who would remain at a base camp and maintain radio contact—could afford it without help.

Kenji thought hard. He needed to raise close to one million dollars. In the early 1990s, Japan's economy was in recession. Many people thought the timing wasn't right for such a trip, but Kenji was not one of them.

He decided to form two committees for what he dubbed "The Antarctic Walk Environmental Research Expedition." One, which he asked future prime minister and avid mountain climber Ryutaro Hashimoto to chair, was the support committee. The other, which he filled with interested researchers, was the science committee, led by Kohshiro Kizaki, Kenji's academic mentor from Okinawa.

With the infrastructure for receiving money in place, Kenji went into fundraising mode, targeting only companies that were doing well despite the recession and those with an environmental bent. He stayed with his friend, professional ghost writer Yutaka Nakamura, who had a small office in Tokyo. Kenji slept on the floor, saving him the hour commute from his parents' house. Nakamura had helped Kenji with logistics on the Africa trip after Kenji stepped into his office on a cold call; Nakamura liked Kenji because he was so different.

"His trip had such a low chance of success," says a smiling Nakamura in a smoky coffee shop in Tokyo, remembering the times Kenji used his office as home. "That character, to try something impossible, is very interesting to me."

Wearing a tie and trying not to sweat through his dress shirt as he visited office after office, Kenji couldn't have been farther from the stillness of Antarctica. But he hustled from company to company and did the best he could.

His success rate was low, getting cash or goods from about 5 percent of the companies he called on. But Kenji swayed a few corporations, among them Amway of Japan, which donated $50,000 in cash and a few of its products, including dozens of chocolate bars.

Years later, the public relations manager and director of Amway Japan, Atsuko Iwaki, a distinguished woman and Boston University graduate, said she decided to sponsor Kenji and his expedition because the company was then initiating an environmental program. Amway Japan, which rivaled and sometimes surpassed Amway USA in sales, had also sponsored the Robert Swan expedition to the North Pole that included Onishi.

"At that time, I was impressed because he was sincere and passionate about the trip," she says in an upscale Tokyo restaurant with walls of glass. "I could feel that he really wanted to go on the expedition. He was living in Japan but you could tell he was a global person."

All of the gear the team members didn't construct themselves, they received from sporting goods companies. Supporters of the Antarctic expedition included Asics (makers of running shoes), Japan Airlines, Nikon, Scandinavian Airlines, Sony, and Matsubara's employer, Sapporo Breweries Ltd.

"Gave us money, and lots of beer," Kenji says. "We don't want to bring beer to [Antarctica]. Just drink. Half of beer, sell it to get money. . . . That was a fun time."

Matsubara agrees that their two years of preparation, with all the men in their mid-twenties, was a "golden age" of their lives. He particularly liked when a few of them would gather around in a Tokyo warehouse after the day's efforts of fund-raising or tinkering with equipment.

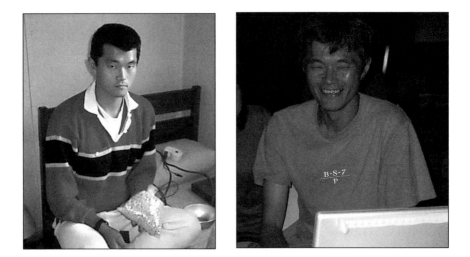

Masayuki Matsubara in the early 1990s (left) and 2008 (right).
Photo on right by Ned Rozell; photo on left courtesy Kenji Yoshikawa.

"We got very close," Matsubara says sixteen years later, in an airy Tokyo bar. "We talked all night, about deep things."

Kenji and his mates raised enough money and gathered enough equipment for the trip. The effort was such that the walk across Antarctica was probably easier for the men than the schmoozing, the tie wearing, and the hand shaking.

"That time was one of my most intense efforts," Kenji says.

■ ■ ■

Antarctica had been walk/skied before, but Kenji had an idea of how he wanted to cross the continent. Shorter routes to the pole are possible, and explorers accept them as Antarctica traverses, but Kenji wanted to go from the Southern Ocean to the middle of the continent by starting at the Patriot Hills camp, which is about seven hundred miles from the South Pole (close to the same mileage one would cover if walking across Alaska). Their base camp was right on the edge of the sea ice, which gave Kenji the feeling of completeness, though not quite as thorough as Roald Amundsen or Ernest Shackleton, who sailed from their home countries to Antarctica. Or, for that matter, the Sourdough Expedition, four men who journeyed by land and river to the summit of the north peak of Denali in 1910. (The north peak is the smaller of Denali's two shoulders, but the one most prominent as seen from their starting point in Fairbanks. As proof of their feat, they left a fourteen-foot spruce pole on the peak they hoped to see from afar. People doubted the Sourdoughs' story until Hudson Stuck, on the first ascent of the south peak in 1913, spotted the wooden shaft through binoculars. It's probably still up there.)

The Antarctic Walk Environmental Research Expedition would be different from all other South Pole treks because of Kenji's desire to perform science all the way. During the trek, he planned to study snow, pristine air, ozone, ultraviolet light, the performance of a gas-detecting patch used in Tokyo, his and his partners' dreams, and, in surprising detail, human waste, which degrades poorly on the cold continent.

Reaching the pole was not one of his main ambitions. He just wanted to draw a meaningful line across the continent along which he could take measurements. And the Amundsen-Scott base at the South Pole made for easier logistics.

"I don't really care about going to South Pole," he says. "South Pole is much easier for pickup."

A year before go-time, Kenji visited the city of Puntas Arenas, Chile. To save the team money, he toured the market there to make sure they had all the ingredients of the Yoshikawa Biscuit, so they would not have to ship biscuits from Japan. He also needed a place to bake the biscuits; he found a bungalow for rent in Puntas Arenas, and reserved it for the next year, when the team would return.

From Chile, he also went to Antarctica, to set up a weather station at the Patriot Hills camp near the Ronne Ice Shelf and to do a topographic survey of the area of base camp. He wanted a year's worth of data to compare with that the team would gather on the traverse. And, with the expectation of learning something in a year, he left a deposit on the rocks near his weather station.

■ ■ ■

The roar of thunder surprised Kenji, Matsubara, and Sano as they began shuffling on their Fischer E-99 skis from their base camp at Patriot Hills, a few Quonset huts rented out by a company based out of Salt Lake City.

"What's that?" Matsubara asked.

"Sounds like thunder, but it can't be," Sano said.

"Must be something in the snowpack," Kenji said.

As they labored on, each yanking a sled weighing as much as an NFL quarterback (and looking as if Tom Brady was under a sheet inside), they heard the thunderclaps again and again. It would be more than a week before they discovered that their collective weight was fracturing unseen layers of windpacked snow beneath the surface. At the start, the noise made them uneasy, and the rumbling was the soundtrack of their dreams as they lay in their sleeping bags.

The expedition was under way. About seven hundred miles, all human-powered, no food drops or chances to refill kerosene bottles. Just three strong men

Photo courtesy Kenji Yoshikawa

Koichiro Harada, then (left) and now (right). Photos courtesy Kenji Yoshikawa.

in their twenties, walking away from two of their comrades—Satoshi Ishimaru and Koichiro Harada—who would stay behind and live at Patriot Hills for two months.

Ishimaru and Harada, an ebullient character who is like a little brother to Kenji, would listen for the radio calls from the trekkers at nine p.m. each day, joke with them to keep their spirits up, and give them weather reports. Ishimaru remembers Kenji as a rare person who follows through on his big dreams.

"He doesn't just think about doing something," Ishimaru says. "He acts upon it more than others. When he is in trouble, he is quick-witted, but not only that, he seems to enjoy it, enjoy the fact that he is facing a problem."

The men would also conduct experiments at the base camp on the nature of ice crystals and snow patterns, and they studied a biological function that was an enduring nuisance in the polar regions, a problem no one had been able to solve. Kenji had an idea about crap, which is why he approached his weather station with interest in what had happened to his exposed movement from the year before. He saw the opposite of the rainforest effect, in which creatures great and small digest human waste within twenty-four hours. With few bacteria or other breakdown microorganisms existing in the below-freezing environment of Antarctica, his pile from a year before was almost identical to a photograph he had taken of it, though some water weight had evaporated. He had anticipated that result.

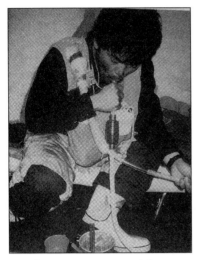

Photo courtesy Kenji Yoshikawa

Back in Toyko, he thought hard. *Every problem has a solution.* He came up with an idea, and it involved his good-natured friend Harada. Harada would conduct a base-camp experiment on the decomposition of human waste. He set up an orange tent that absorbed heat from the sun (which didn't set in the polar summer). Inside the tent were buckets filled with iron powder, sawdust, and hungry bacteria. They also tried buckets heated by a battery for the same purpose. The results of those tests proved inconclusive, as did Kenji's most revolutionary idea—an individual sewage-treatment plant, worn as a vest.

It was Kenji's hope that a person might be able to use body heat to degrade his own excrement and, in the best-case scenario, recover drinking water from it. Harada tested out the system at the Patriot Hills camp. In a report later, Kenji wrote, "The vest processing system worked . . . but was heavy, noisy [due to the air pump] and leaked. For these reasons, quality of life was diminished and restricted when using the vests."

Kenji did not leave the entire study of excrement to his friend. As the men slogged across Antarctica, each of the three teammates would weigh his movements each day and record the result in a notebook. Kenji did this to determine the efficacy of the two-a-day, two-thousand-calorie Yoshikawa Biscuit: were the travelers retaining enough of the superfood?

After detailed study, Kenji determined two biscuits were enough, along with some other foods, to power them through their daily grind across the snow. They would operate at a calorie deficit—it would be hard not to and still carry their food—but they would move for two months, when they would reach the pole and would no longer be limited to a menu they could pull behind them.

Their days became black-and-white copies of the day before, on a landscape that never changed: wake up in the tent, make tea, eat some soup and biscuit, pack up the tent, step into your skis, adjust your salmon-supported waist poles, head toward the South Pole. During a lunch break, sit on your sled, eat more biscuit.

Kenji, the inventor of the biscuit, had less of a taste for it (and, because he was larger of body, perhaps, less of a need for it) than did his partners.

Photo courtesy Kenji Yoshikawa

Sometimes, he didn't feel like eating the biscuit and didn't want to stow the remainder of it. His partners would gobble it up like a dog lurking beneath the dinner table.

"We felt like soldiers in war," Matsubara said. "We were crazy hungry."

Kenji played with the limits of his body. One day, he experimented by eating no food, traveling only on tea. He found that he could keep up with the others while following, but he found leading difficult on an empty stomach. The next day, he ate both his biscuits.

Each man navigated for about an hour at the head of the train, by using the sun and sastrugi patterns (which formed in ridges parallel to the wind direction, toward the pole). Whiteouts forced the skiers to stop, with the leader fumbling for a compass to assure him he was headed true south. During a ten-hour travel day, each skier would lead the pack three times. Kenji often ended up in front at the end of each travel day. He chose the evening's campsite for its suitability for the experiments he repeated each night.

Matsubara and Sano set up the group's triple-wall tent, climbed inside, boiled some water, and transferred the load of their bodies from their legs to their sleeping pads. Kenji stayed outside, taking a snow sample, along with an air sample in a vacuum tube. He measured gases in the air and charted snow patterns. The execution of his scientific tasks cost him one half hour of rest each day.

"No matter how hard the day would be, Kenji would never neglect that routine," Matsubara says.

Photo courtesy Kenji Yoshikawa

In the morning, the men would wake and repeat. Kenji had designed a trip in which they covered about fifteen miles each day, with eight days straight of walking. On the ninth day, they rested. The break from the conventional seven-day week was surprisingly hard on the team.

"God decide every seven days he make rest," Kenji says. "We're on this cycle since [we were] kids. I did a nine-day cycle instead of seven. It's really really painful."

On the ninth day, the men didn't break down the tent. They lounged in their sleeping bags, read books, and for a wondrous change, "eat special food, a treat, not the biscuit," Kenji says. "Noodle soup was heaven."

Kenji napped less than the others. Among other scientific observations, he jotted in his notebook that rest-day bowel movements were 50 percent heavier than those when the men were moving.

He also interviewed his tentmates on their dreams at night, and recorded his own dreams in the same notebook. As the expedition leader, the dreams of his mates gave him some insight as to their state of mind.

"Very easy to tell what they are thinking of me, and each other," Kenji says.

A professor at Kyoto University later analyzed Kenji's dreams as the walk went on. In the early days of the trip, Kenji's dreams most often included, in order, (1) a prizefight featuring himself against a big-name boxer, (2) money, (3) women, (4) food. In the middle days, Kenji dreamed about (1) famous people he admired, (2) foreign countries, and (3) food. During the last two weeks of the trip, Kenji dreamed about (1) the ski across Antarctica and (2) food.

Besides his most frequent dreams of pork-and-noodle soup, Matsubara had a telling dream in which he was struggling up a mountain ridge, moving slowly and cautiously, when Kenji zoomed past him on a motorcycle.

Including the six exquisite rest days, the men walked across Antarctica on metal-edged skis for sixty-seven days. For Matsubara and Sano, who were mountaineers, the experience was not the thrill of kicking toe points into ice and reaching a glorious summit. With the scenery unchanging for much of the route, each man found himself looking forward to the periods when he could follow, rather than lead. There, the mind wandered for hours in a pleasant fog.

"In the mountains, you're in a very beautiful landscape, with a changing view," Matsubara says. "In the South Pole walking there is no danger, no crevasse." (Kenji differs, remembering avoiding harrowing cracks in the ice when skiing from the mountains on the coast to the antarctic plateau.)

Matsubara continues: "In Antarctica, every day was the same, same, same, same, same—for two months. But that sameness was very important for us, because we could think of many things every day. It was like Zen meditation."

With hours of thinking while on the move, the men daydreamed about food other than the biscuit, about their girlfriends back home, and, for about half the time, about where this trip was leading them. They drifted into the soothing rhythm of alternating arm and leg motions, broken only when the leader stopped suddenly to check his bearings. When this occurred, skis slammed into sleds in what each man agreed was his least-favorite experience of the trip: the abrupt interruption from the bliss of entertaining his own thoughts. But the bumps were rare, and the dreams took flight.

"I made a schedule for my life in Antarctica," says Matsubara, who after the trip quit his job as a beer salesman and became a mountain guide.

Kenji too plotted his future while following his mates on the ice cap.

"Think about many things; that's so fun," Kenji says. "All my life's decisions came from that trip."

In the clarity of those hours, he decided he would earn an advanced degree. One day, he would get married and have children. But not before he experienced part of the planet that was missing from his résumé.

"I want to know about this planet, its extreme conditions—desert, polar regions, Amazon jungle," he says. "I never explore the ocean."

The team reached the South Pole on January 16, one day earlier than Robert Scott did eighty-one years earlier (only to find Roald Amundsen had made it

Photo courtesy Kenji Yoshikawa

there first). Before they entered the station, they visited the pole itself, represented by a candy-striped post with a silver orb on top.

There, they paused, each standing on ten thousand feet of ice and snow that presses down on the bedrock of the continent. Sano dug into a remote part of his sled and pulled out a small clay pot. He set the pot down and then covered it with snow. Hiroshi Onishi had reached the bottom of the world.

Because Kenji and his partners had reached the station in their daydreams hundreds of times since about Christmas, each man arrived at the industrial-feeling Amundsen-Scott South Pole Station with a sense of déjà vu. They had rationed well, each with still more than half of his biscuits remaining. Each man had lost about fifteen pounds.

At the Amundsen-Scott dining hall, they ate like the crazy men they were. Their bellies expanded to near bursting; each had to sprint to the restroom more than once. Once purged, their appetites compelled them to return the chow hall and its infinite supply.

"Still, eat again," Kenji says. "Stomach so small."

■ ■ ■

On the eight-hour flight from the Patriot Hills camp to Punta Arenas, in the hum of the DC-6's four propellers, each man became lost, as if he was in his eighth hour of pulling a sled. Kenji pressed his head into his hands and thought about

Photo courtesy Kenji Yoshikawa

the report he would write on all the science they had accomplished, and how the formal document would be a fine keepsake for each of their sponsors. He felt a tingle of pride at having executed the physical part of the journey, and at having new images in his brain to share with a Martian.

He pulled out a notebook to jot down fine details about the antarctic snow he knew he would forget once the plane reached Chile, and especially when they returned to Tokyo, when a few thousand other things would be barking for his brain space.

He flipped his book open to a sketch he had forgotten about, one he had drawn on a rest day. He squinted at the image; suddenly, it called up the virtual map of the world that resides in his head. There on the paper was a sailboat, forty feet long, with a metal hull that could take him from his birthplace in Japan to an ocean so cold it turns to ice.

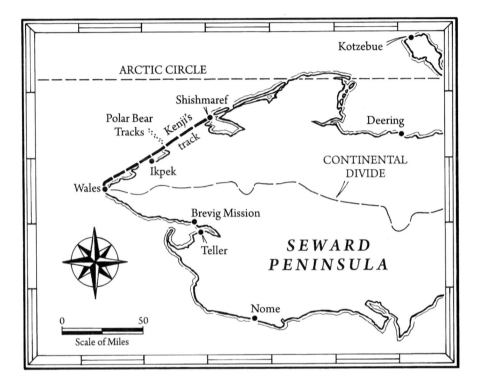

Chapter Ten

The Wine-Dark Sea

Somehow, a few places on Earth have escaped Internet detection. Ikpek, Alaska, is close to being one, but a quick search shows that "Ikpek has no WiFi hotspots."

This is accurate. The ghosted-out Eskimo village is about halfway from eraser to lead along the pencil-shaped barrier islands that extend from Wales to Shishmaref, a living Eskimo village that is our destination for the night. Because eighty trackless miles separate Wales and Shishmaref, and because Kenji wants to drill there today to set us up for an even longer day of breaking trail tomorrow, we ain't stoppin' at Ikpek.

At least Kenji and Tohru aren't. I feel a need to pull over and get a photo of one of those mystery spots on the map, even if it runs counter to my goal throughout this trip, the same one I have every time I go in the field with a scientist—to be as helpful as possible and never be the one who holds up the show. Until now, I have let Kenji out of my sight a few times, but never when we're moving on the machines.

But I can't help myself at Ikpek, which looks like it has a great story to tell. With a single cabin on a snow-covered sand spit connected to a universe of flat white, it could be the movie set for the Loneliest Place on Earth. The cabin is comically drifted, with a flying buttress of snow propping up the leeward side. A few graves in the foreground add depth to a story I won't learn today. The weathered wooden grave markers, with their white paint sandblasted off, conjure the

Ikpek, Alaska

image of people who lived much of their lives here. People who smacked their lips with the musk of seal oil, sons who described to their fathers by candlelight the excitement of the day's hunt, new mothers who pushed through their terror and held a warm, new life to their breasts. Maybe all their years were spent on this grassy, windy hummock of sand, sustained by the protein moving in this far north ocean.

As an Irish French boy born in Manhattan who can never understand the nuances of Eskimo life, it's hard for me to do anything but shiver at the thought of living here. I frame one image on my camera's screen, push the shutter, and hope Kenji and Tohru haven't dropped me.

I turn back to the outer shore of the spit that separates Ikpek Lagoon from the Chukchi Sea, and drive on a line that returns me to the tracks of Tohru and Kenji. Looking ahead, I see two moving objects the size of periods. I gun my engine to gain some ground. The resulting vibration makes me wonder which—my body or the chassis of the machine—will first have a vital part disengage. In fifteen minutes of pounding on concrete drifts, I shave enough ground to discern Tohru's sled as a separate object from his machine. I let up on the throttle. My thumb stops burning.

I don't like this rushing through the country. I prefer skis or foot, going slower but seeing more along the way, but this sand spit on the great ocean is not a place that lends itself to midwinter ski trips. The distance between villages is too far to ski without camping; you could possibly tuck into a fishing shack or shelter cabin between villages to break up the eighty miles, but the exposure here, with few breaks from the gnawing wind, doesn't leave room for a skier's mistakes. With their ability to eat up miles in a few minutes rather than hours, snowmachines and twenty pounds of parka are the common-sense tools of travel here.

And, I remind myself for the hundredth time, this isn't my trip. It's the journey of a man whose mission is to visit as many places as possible in seventeen days, and to perform enduring work in each of them. I'm lucky to be along, even if I miss leading. I would never see this country without Kenji.

As I'm riding, I keep stealing peeks to my left, toward the vastness of the ocean, looking for something I haven't seen in two decades of living in Alaska. Here is my best chance to see a polar bear. Their habitat, sea ice, is the surface supporting our travel, and their main food, seals, live just beneath it. I imagine a bear's tracks would be easy to see out here. Like the prints I just ran over.

I hit the brake on the machine, even though I'm not close enough to Tohru and Kenji to smell the sweetness of two-stroke exhaust.

The tracks are sharp and fresh and larger than my Ice King boots. My daughter might guess they are elephant tracks. They lead from the sand dunes out onto the sea ice. The white bear's prints seem as if they could be steaming, they are so new, but its relaxed gait shows that the bear ambled past hours ago, without the gallop that would have been evident if the animal had sensed Tohru and Kenji.

The bear walked seaward for what looks like forever, until its tracks disappear over the edge of the moon. The great white bear is out there, on that bleached landscape, maybe looking at the black spot of my machine and the smaller one standing next to it.

I strain to see the bear, the one that has surely heard our drone and deemed us something to avoid, but I can't make out anything living on the sea ice. It seems like another planet, like Mars maybe, but this ice covered with snow supports a meat-eater larger than two sumo wrestlers. The bigger an animal is, a visiting lion biologist once said at a lecture in Fairbanks, the more room it needs to survive. There seems to be plenty of room out here, and there must be a good number of seals beneath the ice, which is precisely what these animals might be running short of, especially on the Arctic Ocean north of Alaska.

In a report by USGS scientists a few years ago, they wrote that summer-time losses of sea ice "will require polar bears inhabiting Alaska and Eurasia to either migrate long distances to remain on the ice or spend summers stranded on land." Polar bears would probably not fare well on land. Not because they

couldn't find food, but because brown bears, with a few thousand years' head start living on the continents, would beat them to the food. The researchers concluded that polar bears won't endure if a lack of sea ice forces them ashore in the summer.

Looking out on this endless plain of ice coated with wind-tortured snow, today I'm not worrying about the fate of this polar bear, or its cubs. Ice will touch Alaska's coast during winters for the near future, but people who spend five days a week pondering northern sea ice are not optimistic about its existence in summer later in the century, perhaps as early as 2025.

I squint one last time at the bear track. If worst-case scenarios play out regarding northern sea ice, this might be the last evidence I see of a polar bear. But maybe not. If I've learned one thing in fifteen years of interviewing scientists, it's that there are few absolutes. I want clean answers, but most of them aren't. Especially today, out here, a place where you'd die in an hour if you stripped naked and pondered global warming.

I look eastward. Tohru and Kenji are invisible. I feel a chill of anxiety. *I'm stalling the operation.* I blast off on their tracks, emitting an awful whine, no doubt causing a white bear's head to rise somewhere on the frozen Chukchi Sea. I tear past snow-covered dunes for ten minutes before I see the black dots ahead. They aren't moving, which sends another wave through me.

Shit, they're waiting up.

I motor on and see that Tohru's engine cowling is up. Mechanical problem?

"Lunch break," Kenji says, handing me a foil-covered burrito, heated in an aluminum box clamped to his snowmachine's exhaust pipe. I nod. The motion makes the ice crunch on my beard.

"Thanks. I saw polar bear tracks back there."

"Dang!" Tohru says. "I saw those and wondered what they were."

The snowmachined burrito is underdone, with a hot crust surrounding a heart of ice, but it's nice to eat. I finish mine and notice that Kenji is not eating one. Unlike us, Kenji seems to have no need to eat, drink, or rest. This is our tenth travel day of the trip; it is the second time we have paused on the trail to have lunch.

Shishmaref comes into view as an image for which our eyes are now tuned—dark stubble of single-story buildings on a background of white. We cruise closer to Sarichef Island, part of the same finger of sand spit that extends all the way back to Wales. Our hearts beat faster. At least mine does. I wonder who we will meet, where we will stay, and what the locals will think of us. But the follower's advantage is that he leaves all of the confrontations to the lead man. Kenji will seek out his school contacts and find a place to drill long before we microwave our dinner in the school's kitchen.

We pull up to the school, as usual the largest building in town, and park the machines in parallel. We dismount and follow Kenji inside the building.

Ken Stenek knew we were coming.

"Hey guys. Good trip over from Wales?"

Ken, whom I have met before, is a rarity in these parts—a white guy who calls Shishmaref home, who married a local Native woman, who keeps extending his teacher contract. After his cohorts' terms have expired, he gives them a ride to the airstrip on his four-wheeler. With steely blue eyes and a slightly bowlegged gait that could pass for a local's, the Washington boy found a place that fit him—a place with honey buckets rather than toilets, with a school full of kids who have been his neighbors for years, with the occasional songbird blown over from Asia. Ken, an avid birder, will guide you to it for a fee.

Ken Stenek (right) with scientist David Atkinson

Ken sets up Kenji near a power pole behind the school. It looks like a fine place to drill. Soon, a man with a North Face jacket, knit wool cap with the word "Alaska" on it, and a British accent walks over.

His name is Sam, and he's here to shoot footage for a BBC show about global warming. Ken is his contact in the village, and it's work he takes on often. The *New York Times, National Geographic*, CNN, The Weather Channel, the *New Yorker*—their reporters have all flown to this sandy little island to document how fall storms are eating Shishmaref's northern coast, which seems more vulnerable now than it was fifty years ago, when sea ice formed early and provided a nice cap on the ocean that kept the waves down.

The region including Shishmaref and extending miles inland and east to Cape Espenberg was for centuries the home of the Tapqagmiut, "people along the sandy shore." Shishmaref's location on Sarichef Island was also the site of seal and fish camps in the years before gold and the Shishmaref Post Office, when the settlement became more permanent in the early 1900s.

The fixed location tethered a nomadic people, which is part of the problem in Shishmaref. Built on a barrier island of sand, Shishmaref is doing what barrier islands do—it moves—as storms pick up sand and deposit it elsewhere.

The problem of bad choice of townsite is almost universal in Alaska. Anchorage has an earthquake problem, Fairbanks had a flood issue before the Army Corps of Engineers built a dam upstream, Juneau has homes in avalanche chutes,

Before a 2004 October storm. Photo by John Lingaas.

May 2006

and Yakutat is near a glacier that will someday soon turn one of the world's best steelhead streams into a frigid, cloudy river. Most villages along river systems eventually flood, like Eagle did in 2009.

How do you fix a town with a fatal flaw? In the case of Fairbanks, lots of money, preferably federal, to engineer a solution for the problem and then hire workers to shape concrete to divert natural energy. Several of Shishmaref's man-made solutions—like chunks of rock placed offshore to absorb the blows of the angry sea—have worked for a bit. But the ocean always wins.

Not far from Shishmaref, there is sweet water and protection from the sea at a place known as Tin Creek, about ten miles inland. In 2002, villagers voted to move Shishmaref there. It's a fine idea, as people would have the best of both the land and sea while being protected from storms by the island upon which they formerly lived. But government money has not arrived to fund the move, which the Corps of Engineers estimates will cost close to $200 million. Ken, for one, wants to move to Tin Creek, but he wonders if he will see it, especially in the post–Ted Stevens era. The late powerhouse senator was a big supporter of the Shishmaref move, as he was of so many other Alaska projects that may not come to pass.

▪ ▪ ▪

Kenji woke to the pleasant din of crickets, so loud he couldn't hear his own breathing. He shivered in his light blanket and remembered a few things: he was sleeping on a boat that wasn't in the water, he hadn't showered in days, and he might know the problem with the boat's engine.

Also with him, curled in bunks nearby, were two of his friends and partners in adventure, Hirohisa Shingu and Ken Koizumi. They snored like lumberjacks, having worked until three a.m. after having started their routine of ship repair at eight a.m. They hadn't had a day off in months, not even Christmas. Kenji and his friends were focused on one thing: The Mission.

Kenji, the leader of The Mission, pulled his blanket over his legs. He made a mental note to tell his hard-working friends he appreciated their efforts after the banging of workmen in the harbor would wake them all. When they woke, they could once again progress toward making the *Hoki Mai* the ship that would sail them to a foreign place that would change Kenji's life.

Kenji had no experience sailing in international waters. Though about a decade earlier he had replied to a man featured in a newspaper story because he was giving away a ship to an adventurous soul ("Of course, Kenji got the boat," Kenji's friend Matsubara says), his longest trip with that boat was less than one hundred miles.

This time, he had a dream to sail the Arctic Ocean, the place of Nansen and Amundsen and the other explorers who sought something different and dangerous, an ocean that was navigable for only a few months each year.

First, the team members had to restore the *Hoki Mai*, a forty-two-foot ship with a steel hull that Kenji thought might resist the pounding of the sea ice. His dream was to sail along the coast, cutting a wake that would lasso the great northern jigsaw puzzle of sea ice. His path would take the crew along the coasts of Alaska, Canada, Greenland, Iceland, Norway, Finland, Russia, and then back to the Bering Strait, slipping past the Diomedes and back to Japan.

The trip, Kenji figured, would take a year and a half. Along the way, he would drill holes in the seafloor to document permafrost there, something few scientists had ever attempted, and certainly not in a complete ring around the pole.

Fate seemed on his side. First, a metal-hulled ship had appeared in a boating magazine with the attributes Kenji sought: a ketch about forty feet long, with a steel hull, dual masts for added safety in case one broke, and a faulty engine that kept the price low. A Canadian who had purchased the boat in Vancouver had sailed with it to the tropics for a few years. He landed in Japan to teach English with his wife and take a break. While there, the couple decided to sell the boat.

The ship had a name that caught Kenji's attention: *Hoki Mai*, which in New Zealand Maori means "to return." Nansen's famous ship was the *Fram*, "To move forward."

Their work on the boat was as nonstop as work gets, as Hirohisa Shingu recalled at the site of their renovation, the dry dock in Nichinan, a pleasant fishing village. Nichinan, on the southern island of Kyushu, has spring weather mild enough to dry paint. For that reason, and because Kenji had a friend whose father owned a dry dock there, he chose Nichinan as the place to bring his adventure closer to reality.

Fifteen years after the trip, Shingu, a geological consultant now living in the western Kyushu city of Fukuoka, remembered the mornings in Nichinan: "We may have had a quick cup of coffee but I have no recollection of us eating anything at all," he says, sitting on a wooden plank that helped support the hull of the *Hoki Mai* years ago. "Nothing. We'd get up and go out to work, even without brushing our teeth.

"Our work mainly involved removing old paint, laying down a base for the new paint, and painting over it. So, we'd go out with a grinder in our hands and start scraping old paint away. . . . We'd continue to work till six or seven, and then go eat. For dinner, we'd go to a ramen noodle shop nearby or a Chinese diner a bit farther away and order the same thing every time.

"One hour at dinner was the only break for us, the only time we could forget about work. Only one hour. As soon as we'd get back to the boat, we'd begin our work again.

Hirohisa Shingu, 20 years apart. Large photo courtesy Kenji Yoshikawa.

"The evenings when Kenji would come back with new material [from Tokyo or Sapporo, where he would also meet with sponsors] were the toughest. This is another thing I learned about him—he is a kind of person who has to get things done there and then. When he'd come back with newly purchased material, he'd have to get something done with it right there. One evening he came back from Tokyo and said we'd start soldering and two of us started it right then that evening, a very cold night, till four in the morning.

"We buried ourselves in the work around the boat for six months. So, we knew every cranny and every corner of the boat. We knew the size of every possible space—whether it was big enough to stick our hand in, or whether our whole body would fit in it, or only a finger would fit in. We did everything with its engine as well, so we knew which part had a problem when we'd hear a weird noise."

After six months of grinding and painting and soldering and sleeping in the boat, they were almost ready. Kenji also tended to the finances and the licensing hassles—in Japan, he needed a license for the boat, a different license for operating radar, and a mechanic's license to fix the engine.

Finally, in early April, the men pulled the *Hoki Mai* out of dry dock and rolled the ship down rusty rails into the protected harbor at Nichinan. The orange hull floated, and the boat's diesel engine cranked up when Kenji turned the key.

Photo courtesy Kenji Yoshikawa

Though the crew would later stage a ceremonial start to the journey for television and newspaper crews in Tomakomai, Hokkaido, the first progress of the journey was when the *Hoki Mai* curved around the concrete pier in Nichinan and headed northward. None of the four men aboard (they had been joined by yachtsman Tomoatsu Ohmura, whom Kenji had sought out for boating lessons months earlier) had any experience outside the waters of Japan, but they knew the ship like they knew the bedrooms of their childhoods. With Kenji at the helm, they chugged northward along the coast of Japan.

A problem sprung up even before they left Japanese waters. Rounding Cape Erimo, a town on the jutting chin of Japan's northernmost island of Hokkaido, the *Hoki Mai's* engine sputtered and stopped. The crewmen hurried to unfurl the ship's two sails while Kenji squeezed into the engine compartment to work on the diesel. Inside the swaying, cramped space, he felt saltwater rushes at the back of his mouth and knew he was about to be sick.

His instincts screaming at him to dive into his bunk, Kenji knew he couldn't rest with a disabled engine. He fought through his nausea to troubleshoot the problem. As he was disassembling the engine to get to the malfunction, Kenji dropped a one-of-a-kind screw into the bilge water sloshing around the bottom of the boat. He cursed.

Fishing around the oily, salty water did nothing to alleviate his urge to vomit. He leaned to the side and got it over with. Then he took a deep breath and plunged his hand into the mess to find the screw.

In about an hour of soupy agony, Kenji repaired the engine. He counts that event—with the ship pitching aimlessly in the North Japan Sea and he as seasick as he'd ever been—as one of the most difficult moments of an adventurer's life.

"That was real hard," he says. "It would be a lie if I say I had no fear at all, but I think that you wouldn't even start a trip if you couldn't imagine what it would be like. If you can imagine your trip, you can imagine possible problems that you may encounter along the way."

The engine coughed to life, and the *Hoki Mai* plowed on through the infinite sea. As the days passed, the dream Kenji imagined painted itself in different, unpredictable colors. For every problem encountered, Kenji had a solution. His crewmembers praised his leadership.

"I had gone to mountaineering expeditions before, but Kenji's way of proceeding with a project was new to me. It influenced me quite a bit," says Shingu. "He would obviously make a plan, but he wouldn't let the plan bind him. Kenji's way of planning is very flexible. I had thought you have to stick with a plan, but I learned by watching him that you can change your plan as you go, to suit the situation."

Shingu's most vivid memory of the trip is when the men slipped from Japan northward to the coast of Russia's Kamchatka Peninsula. There, they encountered a violent, heaving storm with a north wind that shoved them back toward Japan despite the engine running at full power and both sails unfurled and tacking into the wind. As the ship rolled crazily, all four crewmembers became sick on the deck. Hirohisa remembers glowing waves that became the enduring image of his trip. "[Phosphorescent plankton] floated away, twinkling with greenish yellow light where the waves washed on the deck," he says. "We'd throw up on them and the waves would wash off the deck. I had watery eyes from being so seasick and yet was so moved by the beauty of those creatures. They were so beautiful! I couldn't tell whether I was a lucky guy or not."

Shingu, who had signed up for adventure, says the trip was "a start of my life, a different life than the one I had been leading up till then. Everything we did back then was exciting. You had to tackle problems that came from unexpected directions and you had to make quick decisions. That training is helping me a lot

Hirohisa Shingu in Nichinan, fifteen years after the launch of the Hoki Mai

in my current job. I really feel like I learned the fundamental attitude about how to tackle unexpected problems. I think all the crewmembers would agree with me."

They sailed through winds, freezing spray, and bulging seas. Past the steaming volcanoes of Kamchatka and the green mounds of the Commander Islands, where Vitus Bering took his last breath. In early July, at the peak of summer warmth in waters so far north, they set a course eastward. They pulled into harbor at Nome, reaching America on July 4th, one month after they had left Hokkaido.

Their first stop in America was not a common point of entry. The men anchored in Nome's harbor and called in the harbormaster on the radio. In halting English he hadn't spoken for months, Kenji explained that they had just arrived from Japan, and he would like for a policeman to sail out to them and check their passports before they walked on American soil.

The men dreamed of cheeseburgers and the other exotic American foods they would eat in Nome as they waited for a policeman. And waited. And waited. A policeman never came and, as evening was setting in, Kenji decided to risk deportation by sailing by himself to shore in the dinghy. He gathered his friends' passports and left the *Hoki Mai*.

On the sands of a Nome beach, Kenji saw a man playing with his children. He approached him.

"Custom?"

"What?" the man said.

"Custom office?"

"Hmmm," the man said. "I'm not sure if Nome has a customs office. Where are you from?"

"We from Japan."

"Wow," the man said. "Never thought I'd see this. Nobody will believe you just came across the ocean. Maybe you should go to the police department, right on the main street of Nome, called Front Street. They might be able to help you there. But I wouldn't expect much today. It's July 4th."

"Thank you," Kenji said with a slight bow. He walked into town, conspicuous in his bright sailing nylons and rubber boots.

After reaching the police station, Kenji explained as best he could that they had just arrived by boat.

"Welcome to America," a policeman said. "But I can't stamp these passports. We don't have a stamp. Just stay out of trouble and enjoy Nome."

* * *

In the land of permafrost—soil still hard as concrete, the result of cold air that pulled heat from the ground thousands of years ago—Kenji soon set to work in Alaska. He and the crew sailed from Nome northward through the Bering Sea and toward the Arctic Ocean. But the summer was gray and short, and the *Hoki Mai* dodged clumps of sea ice that hinted at the difficulties that were ahead in the Arctic Ocean. Before heading farther north, Kenji hooked around Port Clarence and into the protected waters of Grantley Harbor near Teller.

The small community was the same place Amundsen and Nobile had landed in the *Norge*; Kenji felt a sense of history and excitement as he threaded the *Hoki Mai* through the shallow entrance to Grantley Harbor. As he looked at the single-story buildings of Teller and heard the dogs barking in the village, he felt as if he had been there before.

Kenji and his partners spent a month in Teller, living on the boat. They disassembled the large generator that was in the hull of the ship and put it back together outside (it was too large to fit through the hatch). Cruising around Grantley Harbor, the men powered Kenji's heavy drill with the generator and poked holes in the seafloor. There, they looked over the landscape and Kenji pointed out slumping ground that wasn't obvious to the others, features related to thawing permafrost. One of the crew, Tomoatsu Ohmura, remembers this making a long-term impact on him.

"I went to the Arctic and saw with my own eyes the thawing permafrost and thought that something is wrong with the Earth," he said on his home island of Okinawa fifteen years after the *Hoki Mai* trip. "So, I thought it would be fun to establish a new type of farming, a natural way of farming."

Ohmura became an organic farmer on Okinawa, where he recently reflected on what makes Kenji different from other people. "He makes whatever he plans happen," Ohmura says. "When his plan is not possible to accomplish on his own, he involves people around him and makes it happen. Plus, those who get involved feel like they want to help out. What makes him totally different from others is his ability to accomplish what he wants. He never gives up."

After testing the equipment in Teller until September, Kenji and the crew decided to sail up to the northernmost community in the United States, Barrow, where there would be supplies and an airport for the men to fly back to Japan if they chose that option. If they decided to keep moving, Barrow was the first step to boating the Northwest Passage that Amundsen had pioneered earlier in the century.

From Teller, the men sailed into the arctic winter. The *Hoki Mai's* orange bow cut through a skiff of thin ice on most mornings, and the farther north they traveled, the more rafts of sea ice appeared. Huge chunks of ice were also sticking to the shore in some places. It wouldn't budge until the next summer. Kenji knew that his dream of sailing around the Arctic Ocean would have to wait; Barrow seemed a sensible place to wait out the winter.

Nearing Barrow they encountered another storm, which blew in with such force that the *Hoki Mai's* dinghy disappeared. Floating off Barrow, which has no docking facilities, the men wondered if they would ever get ashore, even contemplating having one of them wear a dry suit, jump over the rail, and swim for town.

They decided against that option, and in a few days saw a barge floating into Barrow with the last supplies the town of forty-five hundred people would receive before winter. Kenji sidled up to the barge with the *Hoki Mai*. Two of his crewmen jumped on the barge and went into Barrow, returning later in a borrowed skiff.

With winter closing in and the sea ice growing each day, Kenji planned his stay in Alaska for the winter. In the tradition pioneered by Fridtjof Nansen, he would remain on the ship as it froze in the ocean. The three others on the crew felt they had accomplished their mission. Each purchased tickets from Barrow to

Tokyo. Before they left, his friends helped Kenji move the boat to Elson Lagoon, a protected harbor about ten miles out of town. They sailed in the skinny entrance to the lagoon, and on September 17th at two-thirty p.m., Kenji turned off the key on the *Hoki Mai*'s engine. The silence of the Arctic surrounded them, and all the men yearned for home. Except one.

On September 21st, Kenji's comrades said goodbye. In the Barrow air terminal, Kenji watched his friends board the Alaska Airlines jet bound for Anchorage.

As their plane took off and the deep quiet returned to the snow-covered tundra around the airstrip, Kenji knew he was alone with the *Hoki Mai*, which was freezing fast into the lagoon. After months of nonstop companionship, he was about to enter the most solitary period of his life. And he was delighted.

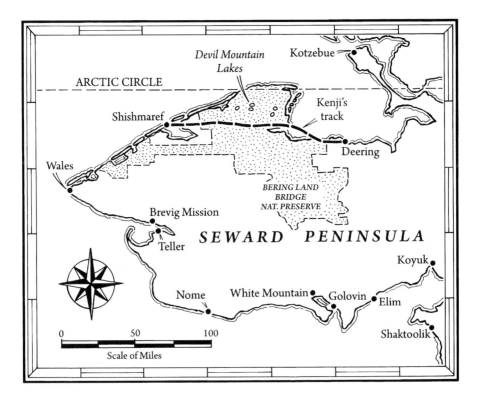

Devil Mountain
Lakes

Kotzebue

ARCTIC CIRCLE

Kenji's
track

Shishmaref

Deering

Wales

BERING LAND
BRIDGE
NAT. PRESERVE

Brevig Mission

SEWARD   PENINSULA

Teller

Koyuk

Nome

White Mountain

Golovin

Elim

Shaktoolik

0   50   100

Scale of Miles

Chapter Eleven

The Night of Winter

As he clomps down the metal-grate steps of the Shishmaref school, Tohru is the first to detect the crime. A red plastic gas can that was strapped to his sled is now tilted in a snowdrift, about twenty steps from where it was last night. He walks over and picks up the jug.

"Empty," he says, holding up the red plastic container. "And another one's missing from the sled."

After a trip that had been free of the third-world experience the teacher in Emmonak had warned us about, we now have another visit to the village store on the day's agenda; we need to replace the fifteen gallons that's now powering something else in Shishmaref.

We drive the machines from the school around the corner to the Shishmaref Native Store. Like a dozen other buildings in Shishmaref, the store is now close enough to the Chukchi Sea that an NFL kicker could boot a football into the ocean from here. And the kick becomes more of a chip shot after each violent fall storm.

From a fuel shack, we refill our jugs and top off our machines (someone had siphoned gas from the tanks as well), and Kenji hands another fistful of bills to the storekeeper. We'll need all this gas to refuel on the snow-covered tundra at least once today before we make it to Deering. The village, even smaller than Shishmaref, is a day's travel away. Kenji, leading the way, will consume even more fuel than an average day because he'll be breaking trail on the longest day of the trip, more than one hundred miles.

■ ■ ■

A few hours out of Shishmaref, with Kenji somehow maintaining a straight line eastward without pausing to look at a map, he pulls over. Kenji reaches into his pack for a camera. He rarely takes photos. So we know there's something unusual nearby.

"Pingos!" he says, pointing out two bulbous hills we just rode past.

I can barely make them out, two white mounds jutting into a baby-powder sky. The ice at the core of the pingos has been here for thousands of years, when the lakes beneath the pingos drained and advancing permafrost infiltrated the previously unfrozen, water-saturated soil, ballooning it upward. Even though we couldn't see them until we almost rode over them, the pingos in better weather are excellent landmarks, visible for miles and miles. Thousands of years ago and maybe last month, hunters used these as lookouts. Kenji found one outside Fairbanks even though it was disguised with a coating of trees. He drilled a shoulder-width hole thirty feet deep into the pingo and dropped an extension ladder into it. The first time I met him, he invited me to climb down and smell the methane emitted from the decaying animals and plants that died there centuries ago. He also spent one summer chipping into a Svalbard pingo with a pick and shovel.

"It was very fun," he says of that experience.

Pingo, Kenji

Kenji's machine soon coughs to life, and he is off between the pingos. Keeping close to my comrades because there's nothing to see in this snow globe, I watch Kenji and Tohru bouncing, sometimes followed by brake lights. I try to throttle down before I hit the same invisible jumps. Driving in this diffuse light is like flying through a cloud, or walking through a strange room in the dark.

The lack of features on this winter landscape makes me wish it were summer. We are entering perhaps the least visited National Park Service entity in the country, Bering Land Bridge National Preserve, and there are some landforms of interest around. Bering Land Bridge is not a stunning place, with its low tundra-and-rock scenery, but it is fitting country for Kenji to be traversing—scientists have called this place one of the Earth's landscapes that most resembles Mars.

The trained eye can discern the volcanic origin of this country beneath the horn of the Seward Peninsula. The Lost Jim lava flow—a shield of gray rock reminiscent of what you see in Hawaii—is an obvious sign of volcanic activity, but of course it is now covered with snow.

Though Jim Beget has perhaps been lost here before, the lava flow is not named for the scientist from the University of Alaska Fairbanks. Jim is a quiet guy who knows a lot and who spends his days reconstructing Alaska's ancient past. Not far from here, Beget and his mentor, David Hopkins, surmised that the roundish lakes in the area are the world's largest examples of maars. A maar (sounds like "Mars" without the s) is a bomb crater blasted when lava hits water. Water is a wonderful fuel for detonation because it expands by a factor of one thousand when it turns to steam. Lava here rose to meet permafrost, which was an enduring source of explosion for as long as the lava flowed upward.

To keep this nontechnical, things went boom, in a big way. The eruptions created the largest maars on the planet. The most striking of those near us is the Devil Mountain Lakes maar. The world's largest maar is shaped a bit like Charlie Brown.

This enduring scar from a colossal explosion twenty thousand years ago is about five miles in diameter, making the system one of the largest bodies of water on the Seward Peninsula. Scientists think the only other planet likely shaped by the marriage of lava and permafrost is Kenji's favorite.

"Mars was the perfect environment to search for the products of volcano-permafrost interactions similar to those found in Bering Land Bridge National Preserve," Beget wrote in a Park Service publication. "Mars, with a mean annual air temperature of –81F, has surface temperatures not that dissimilar to winter temperatures in Alaska." Alaska's all-time low temperature, set at Prospect Creek pipeline camp in January 1971, is minus eighty.

We motor past Devil Mountain and the lakes without noticing them, because we can't see anything we're not driving over. I struggle to stay far enough behind Tohru so that the majority of the air I'm breathing is not oily exhaust. I have no idea how Kenji is maintaining his speed in front and navigating on top of that.

After getting off his machine to scout a steep bank he has somehow detected before plunging over the edge, Kenji leads us down a snow ramp that is almost a cliff. Somehow the machines and sleds cling to the slope for the trip down to sea ice for the first time since Shishmaref Inlet.

We are now traveling on frozen Kotzebue Sound. A peek at the map shows we're on Goodhope Bay, so named by Lieutenant Otto von Kotzebue in August 1816 because, according to Donald Orth's *Dictionary of Alaska Place Names*, "here he had 'good hope' of making important geographic discoveries." Kotzebue, of the Imperial Russian Navy, was looking for the Northwest Passage. He never found it, but he left behind his name on the sound and the town that will be the end of our trip in a few days.

The sea ice of Kotzebue Sound promises better travel than the land, looking smooth and flat and . . . BAM! Before I know what's happening, I am sitting on sea ice, looking west. My machine travels east until the gas fades from my squeeze of the throttle. Like a defiant horse that knows the source of its oats, the machine idles in place twenty-five feet away.

My parka and insulated bibs padded my barrel roll to the snow at seventeen miles per hour. I look behind me and, by squinting, see a coffee table chunk of ice. It acted as a ramp, tipping my sled and bucking me off.

While on my butt, to my great surprise, I hear the whine of a snowmachine. I had thought Tohru and Kenji would be a mile away by now—why would they look back if we've gone seven hundred miles with no troubles? But here comes Kenji. He arrives just as I'm remounting my steed.

"Okay?" he yells over the noise of two machines, giving a thumbs-up.

"Yeah," I shout. "Let's keep going."

As I drive along, I have a flashback to the Brooks Range, where I once worked for a hunting guide. Just when I thought he had forgotten about me, the master guide's Super Cub appeared in the sky. His arm jutted from the window, and he dropped a Ziploc, weighted with rock, containing personal letters and some snacks. When you're not the top dog on a trip, it's easy to think your leader cares only about his mission. But you're not always right.

Late in the afternoon, trails start appearing from the ether, pressed into the snow by machines and sleds. This usually means we are at the frontier of a village network. Tripods of logs confirm that we're getting close.

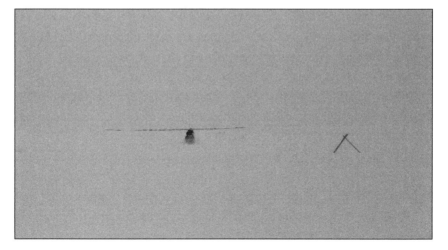

Approaching Deering. Photo by Tohru Saito.

Tohru at the Deering gas pump

Soon, Deering appears. It's the first dark spot we've seen on the horizon for more than five hours of dreamy travel. Kenji again guides us in to the school, located in the center of the village's only street. We clunk up the steps of the Deering school and meet a teacher on his way out the door. Within five minutes, Kenji has set up a place for us to stay and has asked if the gas station is open. It's another long day to Kotzebue tomorrow; we'll need an early start. We don't want to wait for the pump to open. Kenji turns to us.

"Need to go now," Kenji says. "Gas station closes at six."

We zoom down the street, past buildings as drift-burdened as those in Wales. Arriving at the gas pump, we fill up our machines with $5.92-per-gallon gas and marvel at the power of wind to move snow.

With our gas tanks full and machines pulled up under a basketball hoop at the entrance to the school, we spread out our stuff and get ready for a night under desks built for five-year-olds. Before we hit the floor, I have a question for Kenji.

"How did you know where we were going today? I didn't see you checking the map."

"The sun, keep it here," he says, slapping his right shoulder.

. . .

"Oct. 26th—Today . . . we took solemn farewell of the sun. Half of its disk showed at noon for the last time, above the edge of the ice in the south; a flattened body with a dull red glow, but no heat. Now we are entering the night of winter," wrote Fridtjof Nansen in *Farthest North*.

There's a reason ship captains avoid ice like truck drivers swerve from boulders. Growing or blowing sea ice has splintered metallic oak as if it was balsa. Such was the fate in 1879 of the U.S. Navy ship the *Jeannette*, which strayed too far into arctic waters when ice blocked its path southward. The ship froze into the ice east of Wrangel Island, northwest of Alaska. And there she died.

When pressure from ice floes demolished their shelter, thirty-three navy sailors scrambled for the coast of Siberia. Eleven of them made it.

The *Jeannette*'s trip was a stern warning to most mariners, but it was an inspiration to Norwegian Fridtjof Nansen. He heard that villagers on the eastern coast of Greenland had found the remains of the *Jeannette* three years after it wrecked, several thousand miles from Wrangel Island. He had long questioned the prevailing idea that the sea ice on the Arctic Ocean was a rigid cap; he guessed that there was a great polar current that pushed jigsaw pieces of ice continental distances. The wreckage of the *Jeannette*, and the Greenlanders' collections of driftwood that included exotic trees like quaking aspen from Russia, Alaska, or Canada, convinced Nansen that his idea was right.

To prove it, he had a far-out plan: build a ship strong and slick enough to resist the ice, let it freeze in, stay aboard, and see what happens. Pack the ship with five years of provisions and a twelve-man crew. Live on that manmade oasis in the desert of the Arctic Ocean for as long as it took for ocean currents and winds to spit the ship out into liquid water.

Skeptics did not applaud Nansen's plan (they never do), but he had backers. Norway's government chipped in a portion of the money required for the construction of a ship; Nansen donned his suit and called on wealthy companies and individuals for the rest. Soon, he had his money, and his one-of-a-kind ice-proof ship. The *Fram* had a rounded, smooth hull, which would slide upward when pinched by ice rather than being squeezed to destruction.

Nansen and his crew of eleven left Norway in September 1893. They sailed as far north as they could into the ice pack. Within a month, the ship was locked in the ice at about 78° 50' N. The men settled into chores—including a number of daily scientific observations on ice conditions, the activity of the aurora borealis,

The Fram

and the surprising depth of the Arctic Ocean. These readings were maybe the most valuable of the expedition, as they helped to dash the notion that there was land at the top of the world.

With the freeze-up of his ship, Nansen's dream was under way. Following the final setting of the sun, he described the pleasant life onboard the *Fram*:

Tuesday, October 31st— . . . We have good wind for the [generator] now and the electric lamps burn all day. The arc lamp under the skylight makes us quite forget the want of sun. Oh, light is a glorious thing and life is fair in spite of all privations. This is Sverdrup's birthday and we had revolver practice in the morning. Of course, a magnificent dinner of five courses—chicken soup, boiled mackerel, reindeer ribs with baked cauliflower and potatoes, macaroni pudding and stewed pears with milk. Ringnes ale to wash it down.

■ ■ ■

A little more than one hundred years later, Kenji watched from the deck of the *Hoki Mai* as the red ball of the sun melted into a field of white. He turned to face north and saw a sky that resembled a blue-and-pink layer cake. The deep azure that hugged the horizon was the shadow of the Earth. Kenji knew it was the last sunset he would see until late January, and that thought, on November

The Hoki Mai. *Photo courtesy Kenji Yoshikawa.*

17th, filled him with the same giddiness that a plane ticket to the Bahamas might excite in someone else. He was entering his night of winter.

As the light faded, a deep sense of calm enveloped him. Kenji returned to the small cabin of the ship, now frozen in the sea ice of Elson Lagoon. His hibernaculum was a bit tilted due to the uneven freezing of the ice, but he didn't mind. He was alone, he had a project (his PhD thesis), and he had a shelf full of books, including Nansen's *Farthest North*.

"I like to see what explorers did in the wintertime," he says of his library of classics. "It's totally different reading stories about explorers in the polar night, much different reading about them [on the *Hoki Mai*] than in Tokyo."

He was facing sixty-seven consecutive days without direct sunlight, and without the promise of regular contact with those of his species. The human animal was built for life near the equator, for daily doses of vitamin D converted from sunlight via a miraculous process within the skin. Yet some peoples have made a go of it for thousands of years at high latitudes. Kenji was about to become one of them.

"That's the greatest time for me," he says of the sunless period. "Every day, ate from a big bowl of soup, tomato-based. Only thing I eat every day. Always mixing, adding meat. Never need to wash pot."

Photo courtesy Kenji Yoshikawa

His days took on a somewhat predictable pattern of eating, sleeping, gathering snow for water, working on his thesis, and tinkering with an old snow-machine he had purchased in town. He installed a wind generator on the *Hoki Mai's* deck to power his computer. He tried to heat the cabin with free coal he picked from a pile outside Barrow, but its low quality meant he spent whole days just tending the stove. He switched to a kerosene heater, which kept him warm and required little tending. Remembering the igloo the Natives in Resolute Bay helped him build, Kenji constructed an arctic entry of snow blocks to shield the door of the ship.

He knew by then that he would not attempt the ring-around-the-Arctic-Ocean journey he had envisioned for the *Hoki Mai*. Elson Lagoon was the last safe harbor until Kaktovik, a few hundred miles east. And the *Hoki Mai* was a deep-water boat; he had already stuck her in sediment outside Nome and once near Teller where the nautical chart suggested deep water. He thought a different craft would be required for safe navigation throughout the Arctic.

"Tide changes only thirty centimeters," he says, to illustrate that an arctic high tide won't do much to free a heavy boat. "High tide, low tide, doesn't matter. Stuck is forever."

Frozen by choice in Elson Lagoon, when he wasn't working inside the *Hoki Mai* on his thesis, Kenji was taking brief hikes outside, dreaming of a spring

Kenji outside the Hoki Mai. *Photo courtesy Kenji Yoshikawa*

snowmachining trip. He wanted to travel Alaska's northern coast with his drill and look for permafrost on the ocean floor just offshore. Part of that dream was an old Arctic Cat machine he bought from a Native in Barrow.

"Older machine mean easy break," Kenji says. "I learned a lot."

Another thing he learned was not to park his snowmachine on the sea ice next to the boat. The briny ice platform wasn't as solid as it appeared. He discovered one morning that his snowmachine had sunk to its seat in the ice; the ocean had refrozen around it.

"I was very shocked."

Not knowing what to do, he called Barrow on his VHF radio. Within an hour, a half-dozen Native men, part of Barrow's Search and Rescue team, buzzed out to the lagoon. Happy for the task, they chopped his machine from the ice in a few hours, and helped him warm it and then start it up. Kenji was glad for the company, and to learn another lesson. He retrieved a canvas tent from inside the *Hoki Mai* and set it up on the shore about fifty yards from the ship. It became his garage and workshop, which he warmed with a kerosene heater.

Craig George is a biologist who has spent many hours standing atop bowhead whales in greasy boots to learn more from whaling captains about the creatures. In his thirty years of living in Barrow, the former New Yorker had seen nothing like Kenji when George first saw the *Hoki Mai* held fast off Point Barrow.

The Hoki Mai *under moonlight. Photo courtesy Kenji Yoshikawa.*

"We get some oddballs out here," George said at his home in Barrow, the end of the road of North America's settlements. "But as my friendship grew with Kenji, I knew he was the real deal. He was obviously very capable, and he's tough. And he seemed to be honestly interested in the Arctic."

Kenji's existence became somewhat like Nansen's, though much more solitary. With no sun, both men became enamored with the moon. "To console us for the loss of the sun we have the most wonderful moonlight," Nansen wrote. "The moon goes round the sky night and day."

Kenji enjoyed the moon even more than the northern lights. Its predictable trip through the heavens became like seeing an old friend. "It's one of the most beautiful things," he says. "Full moon, light orange, potato shape, the sky completely dark blue. It's a gorgeous picture."

For the first time in his life, the little boy on the bike was 100 percent free. He had no telephone, no email connection, and a VHF radio that allowed him to listen to village chatter when he wished. He ate when he was hungry and slept when he was tired. He had a wristwatch, but it couldn't tell him whether it was six a.m. or six p.m. For most hours of the arctic night there were no time cues from the sky.

One day, after typing on his thesis for hours with breaks only to heat the teapot and step outside, he noticed he was tired. He curled up on his bunk and looked at his watch before he drifted off. It was ten o'clock. He woke with a refreshed feeling, as if he had had a marvelous sleep. He clicked on a flashlight and glanced at his watch. Ten o'clock. There began a mystery unique to his situation.

"How long I sleep? I don't know," he says. "I may just sleep one minute. I may sleep twelve hours. I may sleep twenty-four hours. Maybe thirty-six hours. I don't know really. Still, I don't know the answer today."

Nansen, when ticking off the days of winter in a stone hut later on his *Fram* adventure, wrote of a similar exercise of sleeping through the dark days: "We carried this art [of sleeping] to a high pitch of perfection, and could sometimes put in as much as 20 hours' sleep in the 24."

At other times, like when Kenji was invited to a Christmas party in Barrow, he wanted to keep track of time. He once started his snowmachine and made a trip to the town store just to see what day it was. For the most part, he loved the sensation of living off the clock.

"That's the greatest time," he says. "Time did not control me."

■ ■ ■

Nansen and his men experienced similar freedoms on the *Fram*, though his journal entries reveal an explorer's desire to move. "So it is Sunday once more," he wrote a few months after the *Fram* froze in.

> How the days drag past. I work, read, think, and dream, strum a little on the organ, go for a walk on the ice in the dark. Low on the horizon in the southwest there is the flush of the sun; a dark fierce red as if of blood, aglow with all life's smoldering longings, low and far off like the dreamland of youth.
>
> In the north are quivering arches of faint aurora, trembling now like awakening longings but presently, as if at the touch of a magic wand, to storm as streams of light through the dark blue of heaven, never at peace, restless as the very soul of man.

Kenji fed his sense of adventure by planning for a spring snowmachine trip; Nansen hatched a plan involving the team of sled dogs staked outside the *Fram*. Disappointed that the sea ice in which the ship was locked was drifting away from the North Pole, a point no explorer had then reached, he was prepared to leave the warm glow of his ship and go get it. "A problem that faced this expedition more than any other was that the ship did most of the work," wrote Clive Holland in *Farthest North: A History of North Polar Explorations*. "*Fram* drifted with the current as expected, resisted the ice as expected; she did all that was asked of her, and the crew could only watch and admire. The prospect of five years or more of playing second lead to his own creation clearly discomfited Nansen, and after barely five months in the ice, he began yearning for a more active role. . . . Nansen the hard-headed scientist began to yield without resistance to Nansen the adventurer."

Nansen hinted at his ambition in *Farthest North*:

> Monday, January 15th . . . The longer I wander about and see this sort of [smooth] ice in all directions, the more strongly does a plan take hold of me that I have long had in my mind. It would be possible to get with dogs and sledges over this ice to the Pole, if one left the ship for good and made one's way back in the direction of Franz Josef Land, Spitzbergen, or the west coast of Greenland. It might almost be called an easy expedition for two men.

The easy expedition became one of the more harrowing trips ever laid down on paper, as Nansen did in his lyrical bestseller *Farthest North*. In August 1896, the *Fram*, after drifting for more than one thousand days with the northern sea ice, reached open water at what is now Fram Strait. But Nansen and another crewmember weren't on board for the celebration. More than a year earlier, he, Hjalmar Johansen, and twenty-eight dogs had departed from the frozen ship in an

attempt to reach the North Pole, which was then 450 miles from the ship.

During the five-month trek, Nansen and Johansen skied while the dogs pulled three lurching, four-hundred-pound sleds over sea ice. In the sleds the men carried, among other things, eighty-six pounds of butter, three Norwegian flags, and one nineteen-pound sleeping bag made of reindeer skin, in which both men slept to share body heat. One notable absence in the sleds was an abundance of dog food. "I have weighed all the dogs and have come to the conclusion that we can feed them on each other and keep going for about fifty days."

Fridtjof Nansen

Dog lovers might do well to skip over the part where Nansen and Johansen struggle over rough ice and wet ice and around open leads to get within three hundred miles of the North Pole, but they'd be denying themselves compelling reading. What's it like to travel away from your cozy ship, to which you did not plan to return, and to face daily high temperatures in the minus forties with only your body heat to sustain you? Nansen knew.

> Our clothes are transformed more and more into a cuirass of ice during the day, and wet bandages at night. We crept into the [sleeping] bag to thaw our clothes. This was not very agreeable work. . . . We packed ourselves tight into the bag, and lay with our teeth chattering for an hour, or an hour and a half, before we became aware of a little of the warmth in our bodies which we so sorely needed. At last our clothes became wet and pliant, only to freeze again a few minutes after we had turned out of the bag in the morning.

Nansen and Johansen struggled to within 261 miles of the pole before turning around. Their beasts of burden had dwindled to two when they at last came to an open lead between themselves and Franz Josef Land. They had grown so attached to their last surviving dogs that each man shot the other's.

Upon land at last, even if it was just frozen black rock, the slowness of their travel required them to spend the winter in a stone dugout over which they

Nansen (left) and Johansen (right) after meeting Frederick Jackson on Franz Josef Land

stretched walrus skins. The hut was cramped and cold and the epitome of discomfort, but the two men survived another dark winter, and the next spring skied their way to a chance meeting with English explorer Frederick Jackson.

By sledge and ship, they bumped their way back to Norway and became rock stars. Nansen was a hero in Norway and around the world for returning from one of the last great mysteries on the map. "More was known about the surface of Mars than about the unexplored regions of the globe," wrote Roland Huntford in an introduction for *Farthest North*. "The Arctic was hidden as securely as the dark side of the moon."

However pleasant, Nansen's decompression period was jolting. One evening he found himself wearing a fine suit rather than oily rags that stuck to his skin. He could scarcely believe the President of the United States was raising a wineglass to him, just a few weeks after he was savoring a cold broth of melted snow mixed with polar bear blood. "The ice and the long moonlit polar nights, with all their yearning," he wrote, "seemed like a far-off dream from another world—a dream that had come and passed away. But what would life be worth without its dreams?"

For daring to try, Nansen had won on two counts—he became the man who had traveled farthest north, and his ship proved that sea ice acts more like a living, moving entity than a stagnant cap of ice. He later had the good sense to get out of the explorer business when age made it impractical. He later won the Nobel Prize as a diplomat, a quarter century after the *Fram* expedition.

■ ■ ■

Kenji grew a bit restless on the *Hoki Mai*, but he knew the rarity of this unencumbered time and how valuable it was for someone trying to complete a thesis. Each day, he tapped away on his laptop, ate his stew, and became more scientist than explorer. Almost before he knew it, the horizon was growing brighter in the late mornings. On January 23rd, the sun came up again, casting a pinkish light upon the *Hoki Mai*. Kenji knew it signaled an end to his solitude.

"I am so sad," he says of witnessing his first sunrise in a few months. "This fun time feel like gone. Every day, more sun coming. More spring, more sad."

Kenji says the feeling allowed him to make sense of the counterintuitive fact that the suicide rate of northern peoples spikes in the springtime.

"Wintertime so fun, lots of excuses to stay in," Kenji says. "But when the sun come, all the excuses are gone; have to do something."

Photo courtesy Kenji Yoshikawa

Nansen, when wintering in the stone hut on Franz Josef Land, also lamented the end of winter in a journal entry from February 1: "I have often thought spring sad. Was it because it vanished so quickly, because it carried promises that summer never fulfilled?"

But Kenji was not all glum at the demise of winter. He had planned a spring snowmachine trip with a friend he had made in Barrow. He had his thesis well in hand. And, during the darkness of winter, a female doctor working at the Barrow clinic had stopped by the *Hoki Mai* on a snowmachine trip with two friends. She was the one who had invited him to the Christmas party in Barrow. Arva from California found Kenji interesting but a little odd. He had a feeling she might be his next great adventure.

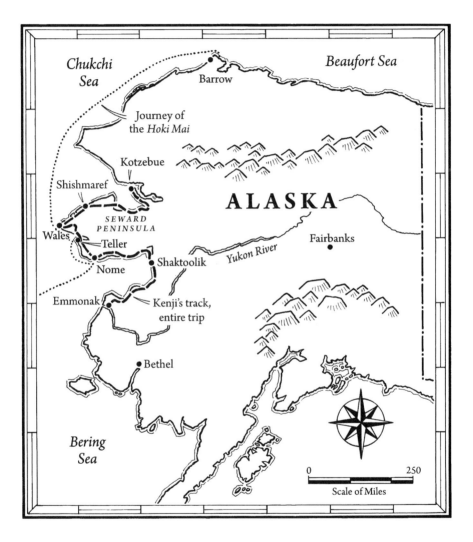

Chukchi
Sea

Beaufort Sea

Barrow

Journey of
the *Hoki Mai*

Kotzebue

Shishmaref

ALASKA

*SEWARD
PENINSULA*

Wales

Fairbanks

Teller

Yukon River

Nome

Shaktoolik

Emmonak

Kenji's track,
entire trip

Bethel

Bering
Sea

0   250
Scale of Miles

Chapter Twelve

Some Kind of Big Changing

Though an adventurer thinks about the end of a journey thousands of times while on the move, reaching a destination is often the trip's most anticlimactic moment. While preparing to lead me across the state from Nenana to Nome on skis, my friend Andy once said, "It's no great shakes getting to Nome."

He was correct. After moving on snow and ice for a month and seven hundred miles, we skied into a gas station on the edge of town and stepped out of our skis in a cloud of diesel exhaust. We then bundled up in wind gear and hitched a ride in the back of a pickup to where we were staying. And that was that.

And so it is here with Kenji. This eight-hundred-mile, sixteen-village trip ends with five bouncy hours on snowmachines, on a day once again so devoid of shadows you could drive off a cliff without knowing it.

Kenji guides us for five sunless hours, this time by "looking at the clouds." After Kotzebue materializes, we arrive at a bunkhouse that Kenji has permission to use. As soon as he pulls in, Kenji jumps from his machine, picks up a shovel, and digs away at a snowdrift pushing against the door.

Tohru and I lurch to a stop and quiet our machines by turning the keys. Wanting to mark the moment of conclusion, I snap a photo of Tohru.

We are done. Our thoughts drift from the unknown of tomorrow's trail to people waiting for us at home. My wife has informed me that one of our dogs is about to die, so that punch to the gut is waiting. Kenji and Tohru also have long pulls on the phone inside the bunkhouse. I see them nodding while looking out the windows at

Approaching Kotzebue

the whiteness of spring, remembering what they left behind a few weeks ago. Life on the trail fades like the last ice crystals clinging to pungent April soil.

But the trip is not over yet. For another step in the process of decompression, we drive our machines over glazed and graveled village streets to something we haven't seen since Nome—a restaurant. Over plates of cheeseburgers and French fries that are not microwaved, we lift plastic tumblers of Coke and click them together to mark the end.

Despite the missing equipment that never caught up with us, Kenji has poked more than a dozen holes into western Alaska, and his thermisters are now performing their work. His dream is that they will endure long after he is gone, and that village children who are tomorrow's elders might choose to use them, to see how their home has changed. Or hasn't changed.

Kenji's legacy now sits quietly in tundra throughout rural Alaska. He is already thinking of other Alaska villages he will visit. Before the year is over, he will travel to almost every village that has permafrost, and some that do not. Later in the year he will note in his blog a milestone as he stops at a school in Interior Alaska, traveling in his pickup truck:

> I should have small cerebration today in Tok. Since morning, I am driving and drill-
> ing crazy as usual. Finally we reach 100 schools today!! I remember Doug Goering

Tohru, Kotzebue, March 29, 4:42 p.m.

Kenji and Tohru, Kotzebue

and myself start drilling at Pearl Creek Elementary, Fairbanks in 2005. It takes three years to reach 100. It was really really fun to meet students, teachers, principals. Also I was very exciting to see new village. Not just seeing village as geography also we have to drill, this is good part! We understand thermal condition of the area too!! What wonderful job!

. . .

Inside the warm cabin of the *Hoki Mai*, Kenji paused while using the WordStar program to tap out his thesis. He held his breath, straining to hear a whine that could have been that of a cat pawing at the door. It wasn't the polar bear, the one that stood on its hind legs to peer into the porthole a few days earlier. This purr was different than the howl of the wind and the flutter of the wind generator's petals. Yes, there it was. A snowmachine. No, two. He scrambled for his parka.

The riders had not expected to see an orange sailboat listing in the ice of Elson Lagoon. They were on a ten-mile ride from the town of Barrow to Point Barrow, the northernmost wedge of land connected to the United States. As the rest of America prepared for Halloween, a stinging breeze made Barrow feel like it was twenty below.

One of the travelers, a pharmacist at the local hospital, had misjudged the wind in choosing his boots for the day. His feet were chilled to the point of numbness. He and his two companions were happy to see a dark figure emerge from the igloo at the boat's entrance and wave them inside.

The three travelers—the pharmacist, a doctor's wife, and a female doctor named Arva—squeezed into the cabin of the *Hoki Mai*. They savored the cubby's heat, enhanced by several computers Kenji had running. The contrast between the boat's interior and the first bite of arctic winter had a stunning effect, as if the travelers had stepped into a lunar module.

Kenji had a pot of coffee brewing from a handy packet of grounds before the three had pulled off their jackets. With everyone settled in the cramped cabin, he offered a treat.

"M&Ms?" he said, passing a king-size bag to Arva. She poured some into her palm as the pharmacist removed his boots.

"Thanks for waving us in," he said. "It's pretty wintry out there."

"No probrem," Kenji said, smiling.

Kenji and the Hoki Mai, *Elson Lagoon. Photo by Frederic Moras.*

Kenji hadn't practiced his English for a while, so the group communicated as they could, fleshing out some answers with pantomime and by pointing at maps.

The three travelers all lived in Barrow but—like most people in town—had no idea a man was out there on the ice. But here he was in a comfy cocoon amid a landscape that would kill an unprotected human as fast as someone who fell to the surface of Mars. It was like nothing Arva, of Walnut Creek, California, had ever seen.

"Where are you from?" she asked Kenji.

"Japan," he said. "Came in here few weeks ago."

The travelers learned he was working on his college degree, but they couldn't discern what exactly he was studying. Kenji, as best he could, asked them who they were.

"Where you originate?" he asked Arva, wondering if she might be an Eskimo.

"California," she said. "But my parents are from China."

Kenji filed that information away in the back of his mind and poured a last cup of coffee for his new friends.

With the blanket of darkness covering the day, the travelers thanked Kenji and clunked back into the wind in their heavy gear. He closed the hatch behind them and was alone again with his computers and his stewpot and his thoughts. They motored back to Barrow with an interesting story to tell of an odd fellow thriving out there among the seals, polar bears, and arctic foxes.

Arva returned to her apartment in Barrow, a three-bedroom that felt a bit too spacious. At work the next day, she told her friends Lyn Kidder and Frederic Moras about Kenji. Lyn, a part-time writer who worked in the hospital lab, and Frederic, a photographer who worked odd jobs in Barrow, thought Kenji was a great story. A week later, Arva guided Lyn and Frederic back to Kenji.

Lyn, who now lives with Frederic in Ruidoso, New Mexico, remembered her first impressions of this unusual character. "Amid all this white sky and white ground, there's this orange sailboat sitting there," she says. "There it is, on the lagoon side, frozen in the ice. A spaceship couldn't have looked weirder."

The leaning orange ship, with its generator blades whirring and scientific instruments extended on frosted white masts, reminded Lyn of a Dr. Seuss book. Then she saw Kenji. "As we pull up, this Japanese man comes out, all dressed in fur," she says. "It was so bizarre."

Kenji was wearing pants made from the skin of a sled dog that died of old age in Greenland. Also from Greenland was his caribou-skin parka. Using the hide of a polar bear he received from a Barrow Native, he made a large pair of mittens. His goal was to have clothes that would allow him to lie comfortably on the ice, like a polar bear waiting for a seal.

As they settled into the cramped cabin, Lyn gave him a few gifts of food, including a super-size bag of M&Ms. Kenji told her his story of coming over to Alaska from Japan, which she found amazing. He didn't mention his other journeys over the skin of the planet, though she would learn about them later.

"He hardly talked at all about his experiences," she says. "He doesn't blow his own horn."

As the party was leaving Kenji's boat, Frederic, a friendly, thoughtful man, turned to Kenji. "We live in hospital housing and have plenty of room," he said. "Come stay with us when you need a shower, or just some time away from here."

Kenji nodded and smiled. His new home base in Barrow would lead him places he couldn't yet imagine.

Arva had an idea just before she left the boat. "We're having a party on Christmas Eve," she said. "You should come in for that, too."

That invitation later caused a minor quandary for Kenji, who often couldn't tell a.m. from p.m. during the perpetual night. "Got closer to December 24, I don't know which day I am," he said. "That's a little problem. Sometimes I had to go into village to see which day this is."

■ ■ ■

Arva had become a doctor in Barrow at about the same time the *Hoki Mai* reached America at Nome. She had first tasted what Alaska had to offer while doing work at the Sitka hospital. She had met Lyn and Frederic there, and the pair later moved to Barrow. Arva moved to Barrow because Lyn and Frederic said good people lived there, because she thought it would be interesting, and because service there would help her pay off her student loans.

Arva had purchased a snowmachine on the way up to Barrow during a layover in Anchorage. She had no experience with the ubiquitous Bush tool and plaything, but she knew Barrow didn't have many roads and wanted the freedom of getting out of town.

"I thought it would be fun to check out polar bears and things," she says.

Her snowmachine carried her to her future husband, but she never dreamed of that outcome.

"They [Lyn and Frederic] were key in getting me to Barrow, and then befriending Kenji, so that he always came to the hospital when he came into town," Arva says. "If it wasn't for that, we probably wouldn't have hooked up. This one-time meeting with somebody on a boat from Japan just wasn't going to do it."

"We were definitely facilitators," Lyn says.

For his part, Kenji liked what he saw in Arva—an attractive, independent woman who was respected among her peers. And, hey, she owned her own snowmachine. On his visits to the hospital, he made it a point to always walk past where Arva worked. Lyn remembers how she detected Kenji's presence even before she saw him. "I could always tell when he was there because there was the smell of fuel oil in the halls," she says.

While taking showers and washing his clothes at Lyn and Frederic's hospital housing, Kenji also met another doctor, Paul McCord, who was from Chicago but was learning to love life in the Arctic. Paul admired Kenji's achievement of sailing to Barrow and his apparent talent for fixing his snowmachine. Kenji's seemed to break often, but was never down for too long.

When Kenji dropped by the hospital, Paul would always ask about trail conditions. Sensing a kindred spirit, Paul asked Kenji, mostly by running his finger across a map, if he might want to try a spring snowmachine journey. Paul had traveled to Fairbanks to meet with Roger Siglin, inventor of the sled Kenji is currently using and a veteran of thousands of miles of arctic travel. He came back even more enthusiastic about traveling the landscape.

Kenji had unfinished work in Teller drilling for permafrost under the sea surface, so Paul proposed going there. Though he didn't trust his machine, Kenji agreed, in part because he knew if he didn't go, Paul would go alone.

The two met out in Elson Lagoon, next to Kenji's boat, and they timed themselves in constructing an igloo that was large enough that a snowmachine could fit inside (should they need to repair it on the trip).

Kenji and Paul struck a fast friendship. Paul grew so accustomed to the cadence of Kenji's English that he found himself interpreting for others. When traveling together on fun trips to neighboring villages, the pair didn't need words; a wave or a nod would suffice. As far as Kenji's romantic future went, it also didn't hurt that Paul's wife was Arva's good friend.

■ ■ ■

When Kenji and Paul made their trek to Teller—a major undertaking by snowmachine including hundreds of miles of windblown tundra and a traverse of the Brooks Range—Paul's snowmachine broke outside Point Hope. They towed the machine in and ordered a part to be flown in to the village. Much to the amazement of their trip followers back in Barrow, who got updates from the pair via village phone, Kenji fixed the machine. They made it to Teller.

"He seemed to be a jack of all trades," Arva says. "My first impression in the boat was 'he's eating good, and he can cook.' And then he's obviously intelligent with all those computers and working on his PhD. And he's a good mechanic. He's got a lot of talents."

The pair had known each other for just a few months, but neither Arva nor Kenji was an indecisive person, and they both somehow knew they had found the right person.

"He knows what he wants in everything," Arva says. "He's not very wishy-washy, and he doesn't like that in a person either. You make a decision and that's your decision."

Arva's parents knew their independent daughter would do as she wished, but they made the request that she and Kenji travel to China and meet with her grandfather. If Kenji was okay with him, they reasoned, they would give their blessing.

On a trip to Thailand, Arva and Kenji made two diversions—one to Tokyo, so Kenji's parents could meet her, and another to China,where Arva's grandfather lived.

Arva, Maya, Kent, and Kenji, in Valdez. Photo courtesy Kenji Yoshikawa.

In a small traditional home with bamboo mats on the floor, Kenji pulled up a chair next to Arva's grandfather. He wrote Kanji symbols on a notebook, and Arva's grandfather responded in kind. They used maps to convey the rest. The old man admired Kenji's spark, and later communicated that to Arva's parents.

"Then my family warmed up to it," Arva says.

Less than a year after Arva first saw the orange sailboat in Elson Lagoon, they were married near Palo Alto, California. Paul McCord was Kenji's best man.

In the most emotional period of their early time together, when they were in Hokkaido as Kenji finished his PhD, Kenji and Arva heard that Paul had disappeared on a solo snowmachine trip while attempting to reach the village of Wainwright, about one hundred miles from Barrow. When they heard Paul was missing, Kenji wanted to jump on the next plane out of Sapporo to search for his friend. But after conferring with Arva and realizing there was probably little he could add to a mission that already included a helicopter, he stayed in Japan. They both mourned his loss when the news came a few days later that Paul's snowmachine had been found in an open lead of the Arctic Ocean. Searchers never found his body.

With marriage came a drastic shift in lifestyle for the couple, especially for the world adventurer. When Arva's term in Barrow ended, they moved to Hokkaido, where Kenji finished his schoolwork and they heard of Paul's death. They then moved back to Alaska, buying a house and land outside Fairbanks.

There were still a few items to tidy up in Barrow. Kenji returned there and got the *Hoki Mai* on an empty barge headed to Seattle; he would later travel there to convert it to more of a pleasure craft fit for a family. The *Hoki Mai* is now docked in Valdez, about a seven-hour drive from Fairbanks, where Kenji and Arva live with the greatest agents of change and discovery a human being can experience: Maya, who shares her father's instinct to be a leader, was born in 1999. Kent arrived two years later.

"From single-man exploration to working with sponsorship to team-oriented expeditions to family," Kenji says. "That's some kind of big changing. I'm still in the middle of that. I don't know what the next big changing is, maybe Tunnel Man."

Epilogue

Finding Mars

Asnow squall spits white nickels from a sky painted battleship gray. Sandhill cranes fly north in an arrow thrown from the Great Plains, croaking in prehistoric formation. The air smells like damp spruce on this early spring night in one of the state's smallest villages, on the shore of its largest lake, where the ice hisses as it rots. Sixty-four people live here in Igiugig, a place where a fifteen-minute stroll completes a tour of the two downtown roads.

Kenji landed here minutes ago, a passenger in a chartered Cessna 206. He walks the gravel road to the Igiugig school (home of the No-See-Ums). As he presses into the soft rock with his prizefighter's stride, a pickup approaches from behind. Its cargo is six little girls, about one-third of all the No-See-Ums. The girls are headed for some after-hours activity at the school.

As they pass Kenji, he waves.

"Kenji!" a girl says. "Tunnel Man's here!"

Their laughter peals through the village, a dozen frame houses perched above the Kvichak River. The Kvichak, as clear as mountain air, drains Iliamna Lake, which is deeper than many ocean bays and has a legend of a sturgeonlike monster lurking its depths. In a few months, sockeye salmon, looking from shore like dirigibles floating in air, will clog the great lake's connection to the sea.

It is late April, two years since Kenji's snowmachine trip from Emmonak to Kotzebue. He has asked me along on another of his spring trips. He is using the sky this time, chartering a ride from Wright Air Service in Fairbanks. A seasoned

pilot, Dave Lorring, is finding holes in the weather to suit Kenji's ever-changing schedule. Kenji would rather be snowmachining, but an aircraft the size of a large pickup truck gives him the ability to visit more villages each day.

Kenji has planned this trip by Cessna despite the little-known fact that motion sickness is Tunnel Man kryptonite. His secret defense is a pill, manufactured in Japan, that he swallows half an hour before flying. Kindly, he also handed a package of the pills to me before we took off from the East Ramp of Fairbanks International. They seem to be working. Neither of us has reached for the Ziplocs Dave has placed in seat pockets for us.

Today began in Bethel. After we had breakfast there with a friend Kenji had met at a teachers' gathering in Fairbanks, the Cessna's wheels touched gravel in Crooked Creek and Sleetmute above bends of the Kuskokwim River, and again at Koliganek and New Stuyahok on the Nushagak River. Counting a stop at Iliamna to fill the Cessna's wing tanks with gas, Igiugig is our seventh village of the day.

This has been easy day by Kenji Crazy Trip standards—he has drilled a permafrost observatory at just one site, New Stuyahok. At the other villages, he downloaded data from holes he had drilled on previous trips; from those places, we were airborne less than one hour after the Yoshikawa Hit and Run.

He spoke to students at one school, Koliganek, and showed them Tunnel Man episode one. While the video played on a whiteboard, a Native girl of about sixteen turned her head several times between the screen and the bald, broad-shouldered Japanese man in the back of the room. She smirked as she put the two together.

Kenji and pilot Dave Lorring on the boardwalk in Nightmute

Despite the uncoolness of giggling, each of the fourteen Native kids laughed at some parts of the Tunnel Man video. None of them slept, or fought, or moved around, like the kids were doing at a village a few years ago, in a moment that inspired Kenji to create Tunnel Man.

Back then, he had just purchased an iPod nano. He marveled at its video function, remembering the effect music had upon him as a teenager. He saw in his hands a way to reach kids who would ignore the scientist who offered them nothing but words. He has made four Tunnel Man videos, and is working on a fifth. When he shows more than one episode in a classroom, he asks the kids which format they liked best—the rapping Tunnel Man or the goofy Tunnel Man dressed in a sombrero and lip-syncing to a Latin beat? He is always refining the product, never quite done.

"My dream is to go to a Native village and to pass kid with Tunnel Man on his iPod," Kenji says.

Teachers seem to appreciate his efforts. On this trip, we have stayed overnight in Bethel with the teacher Kenji met in Fairbanks. When he heard she lived in Bethel and worked with kids, he enlisted her as part of his team.

"Kenji has a unique enthusiasm—such as his willingness to dress as a super-hero," says Andrea Pokrzywinski, who teaches science classes via a live Internet feed to students in the Lower Kuskokwim School District, a West Virginia–size swath of twenty-eight village schools in one of the poorest regions of Alaska. "It draws kids' attention to see something that extreme. . . . And it's not everybody who pulls up in a snowmachine to work with the kids. He's always searching for a new, creative way to reach kids. My students don't read text well—they're much more visual."

Kenji's alliance with a teacher who can help him spread the Tunnel Man message shows off one of his understated strengths—he is fearless in asking for help when his task requires a skill he doesn't have.

"Most of us, for one reason or another, don't make friends with everybody we meet, but he's managed to make friends everywhere he goes," says Glenn Sheehan, the director of Barrow's Arctic Science Consortium who has known Kenji since the *Hoki Mai* days.

Here in the Koliganek classroom, the teenage boys are tall, angular, and athletic. Any of them would smoke you in a game of one-on-one. They like to hunt for moose and eat salmon and any bird they can catch. A teacher whispers that these kids are not good readers, that they will never be academic stars. Attempting to reach them with Western methods is often a waste of his time. If any of them go to college, they will surprise their parents and teachers, he says.

Standing there in the back of the classroom, however, a person sees that Kenji has the attention of these boys and girls. They will remember who he is. Some will, in a few weeks, months, and years, recall what he is doing.

Kids watching Tunnel Man in Chefornak, Yukon-Kuskokwim Delta, population 394.
Photo courtesy Kenji Yoshikawa.

"He makes dirt and ice interesting for the kids," says Mark Battaion, a teacher in Igiugig who has devoted a strip of wall to "Kenji's Permafrost Chart." "He also brings in that cultural thing of being Japanese. Kids in the Bush have similar features, and we study a lot of eastern cultures."

Battaion and his wife have spent a few years in Japan. He notices Kenji's upbringing in his work. "He's typical Japanese in some ways—when they choose to do something, they go 110 percent. The videos are typical of what you see in Japan. His ability to get kids interested in the media of video is better than just him standing there yakking."

While Kenji is indeed blasting through these villages and popping in on teachers with minutes of ready-for-me-or-not warning via his satellite phone, he doesn't seem to be doing it to push new thumbtacks into his Alaska map. He gives each lecture with similar energy, even if he's on his third village of the day. And, unlike some adventurers who truly love the people they visit in the moment but never contact them when the trip is done, Kenji invites the kids to climb Mt. Kilimanjaro with him this fall (where he drilled for and found permafrost near the summit a year before). He also tells the teachers to bring their kids to Fairbanks and he will take them on a tour of the U.S. Army's permafrost tunnel, a stinky-from-the-decay-of-exposed-mammoth-flesh place students won't forget. Last year, a teacher from McGrath stayed at Kenji's house when she came in from the

Calling for a ride in Kasigluk

Bush; she recovered in the Yoshikawas' spare bedroom after giving birth to her first child at Fairbanks Memorial Hospital.

"A lot of people blow through the villages and never come to the school," says Battaion, who has taken Kenji up on the permafrost tunnel tour when he brought a few Igiugig kids up to Fairbanks. "He takes the time to visit with them, and they really like him."

. . .

This Cessna trip with Kenji has been exhausting, both for the number of villages visited per day and the distance covered (mileage for the five days equals a trip from Fairbanks to St. Louis). The pilot and I and Kenji have missed several lunches due to the schedule, and Kenji, who assembled just-add-boiling-water food for the three of us in an ActionPacker, didn't toss in any oatmeal packets or anything else resembling breakfast.

But you don't expect fine dining on a trip with Tunnel Man. You expect adventure. And he delivers it, from the moist air of Chenega Bay in Prince William Sound to the sunny boardwalks of Nightmute in western Alaska, where Kenji pokes his head into a sauna because he sees inky smoke coming from its stovepipe. He meets an elderly woman inside who explains that—because Nightmute has no trees larger than gnarled alders that grow on the hillside—she is firing her sauna's barrel stove with old clothes soaked in seal oil.

"These are the best," she says, holding up a synthetic work boot that would seem to contain plenty of toxins along with its British thermal units.

During the trip, I think of a few questions I haven't asked him before. The first is, why doesn't Kenji become a pilot? His answer: he really doesn't trust planes, and then there is the recurring motion sickness. On a walk from the airstrip to Nightmute, I ask Kenji the second question: does he want to go to every village in Alaska?

"Yes," he says. "Or else I feel shame if someone says a name [of a village] and I don't know where it is."

He wants to look at the map of Alaska and have an image pop in his head for every place-name out there. Eek, yes. Nunam Iqua, check. Platinum, been there. Igiugig, one of his favorites.

Since I last traveled with Kenji, he has almost pulled off the feat—with the exception of southeast Alaska (for which he has a plan that involves a boat)—of going to every place in the state that has enough kids to merit a school. Maybe some

Nightmute "steam"

pilot who has bumped around to jobs with different air services in various regions of Alaska has seen more villages, but there aren't many of those men around.

Kenji has stepped into these places in just a few years, and he keeps coming back to Faro and Fort Yukon, to Kaltag and Kotlik, to download his data and speak to students. And the latter is not an easy thing for him, with an accent that I find somewhat difficult to understand when I haven't seen him for a while.

"I don't know how many percent kids can understand," he says. "But if I speak, I can succeed."

■ ■ ■

For all his extrahuman energy and efficiency, Kenji is now in his late forties, and, as Mick once sang, time waits for neither the slackers nor the exceptional. The little boy who wanted to go to Mars will probably never get there. Kenji has studied Martian permafrost and is an ideal candidate for such a mission, but, for all his drive, even he can't overcome Earth's gravitational pull. Space agencies that once had Mars on their mission schedules have backed off.

Spend some time with Kenji, though, and you get the sense that walking on Mars doesn't matter much to him, perhaps not as much as it did a few decades ago. Maybe, after leaving footprints on Sahara dunes and wincing as the antarctic

Behind Shageluk school

wind nibbled his cheeks and eating fish heads in the jungle and groggily watching luminescent waves wash over the deck of the *Hoki Mai* and witnessing the messy, wonderful emergence into the world of two human beings, he has seen enough to give a Martian a good briefing about what his home planet is about. And, maybe, in this landscape buckled with frost polygons that still hold the cold from twenty thousand years ago, Kenji has found his Mars.

Rich man! My Russian friend told me that "rich man" means not by material nor money. People had a lot of memories, experience. These people will be Rich Man! I completely agree about this! I would like to be a rich man so that we have to keep challenging new. . . .

I sold my sail boat this week. I keep her since 1993, I left Japan with her, spending arctic winter with her and to meet many people in her cabin. I had a lot of memories with her. But my mission with this ship is over. So I should go next step (e.g. next challenge).

—Kenji's blog entry for June 20, 2010

References

Pages 33 and 34, quotations from *Klondike: The Last Great Gold Rush, 1896–1899*, Pierre Berton (Random House Canada/Anchor Canada, 2001).

Page 72, quotations from *The Long Exile: A Tale of Inuit Betrayal and Survival in the High Arctic*, Melanie McGrath (Alfred A. Knopf, 2007).

Page 92, quotations from *My Life as an Explorer*, Roald Amundsen (Amberly Publishing, 2009).

Page 93, quotations from *Alaska's Daughter: An Eskimo Memoir of the Early Twentieth Century*, Elizabeth Bernhardt Pinson (Utah State University Press, 2004).

Page 111, quotations from *America's Forgotten Pandemic: The Influenza of 1918*, Alfred Crosby (Cambridge University Press, 1990).

Page 114, quotations from *Flu: The Story of the Great Influenza Pandemic of 1918 and the Search for the Virus That Caused It*, Gina Kolata (Touchstone, 2001).

Page 120, quotations from *Hawk's Rest: A Season in the Remote Heart of Yellowstone*, Gary Ferguson (National Geographic, 2003).

Page 159 and beyond, quotations from *Farthest North*, Fridtjof Nansen (Random House, Modern Library Exploration Series edition, 1999).

Page 160 photo is from *Farthest North: Being the Record of a Voyage of Exploration of the Ship Fram 1893–96 and of a Fifteen Months' Sleigh Journey by Dr. Nansen and Lieut. Johnsen with an Appendix by Otto Sverdrup Captain of the* Fram, vol. 2, by Fridtjof Nansen (Archibald Constable and Company, 1897).

Pages 165 and 166, quotations from *Farthest North: A History of North Polar Exploration in Eye-Witness Accounts*, Clive Holland (Carroll and Graf Publishers, 1994).